WE LIVE IN SOCIAL SPACE

A Window to a New Science

Fred Emil Katz

authorHOUSE®

AuthorHouse™
1663 Liberty Drive
Bloomington, IN 47403
www.authorhouse.com
Phone: 1 (800) 839-8640

Published by AuthorHouse 02/02/2017

ISBN: 978-1-5246-5974-5 (sc)
ISBN: 978-1-5246-5973-8 (e)

Print information available on the last page.

Any people depicted in stock imagery provided by Thinkstock are models,
and such images are being used for illustrative purposes only.
Certain stock imagery © Thinkstock.

This book is printed on acid-free paper.

Because of the dynamic nature of the Internet, any web addresses or links contained in
this book may have changed since publication and may no longer be valid. The views
expressed in this work are solely those of the author and do not necessarily reflect the
views of the publisher, and the publisher hereby disclaims any responsibility for them.

CONTENTS

FOREWORD

Thanks to the revolution of information transmission, we live in a whirlwind of connectivity. There is seemingly no limit to who can connect with whom. Distance is no longer a word that has meaning. And place seems a quaintly irrelevant term. When we are within reach beyond the here, there seems to be no here. There is only connectivity. Only fleeting, ephemeral connectedness without duration seems real. Indeed, "duration" is another term that has vanished from our life.

Taking a step back from this picture of modern woe, what are we missing in our disgruntled despair? Is there a location, amid our connectedness, where we are we? Where we are here? Where we are? Do we have any kind of grounding? Is there, after all, something real that underlies human social living no matter how ephemeral and fleeting are its manifestations in our daily life?

I suggest that one can conceive of Social Space as the base camp in which we actually live our lives, regardless of the seemingly fleeting character of our daily life. The nature and content of that Social Space can be discovered. The following pages describe some steps to do just that.

I am guided by two mottos:

Alfred North Whitehead's theme that
Science is Adventure of the Mind

and

President Franklin Roosevelt's "We have nothing to fear but fear itself" – modified to *We have nothing to fear but our mental shackles.*

This book is dedicated to the memory of Ted Levitt, my cousin

He was passionate

>   In his embrace of reason and the mind's creativity

>   In his teaching

>   In his writing

>   In his devotion to family; I know – I was a beneficiary of his many versions of that devotion.

He was humanity at its best.

Ted was a prominent professor in the Harvard Business School. His parents sponsored my coming to America when I was nineteen years old. At that time Ted, himself an undergraduate working his way through Antioch College, encouraged me to go to college – and did things to make it happen.

Introduction

Does the fetus know it is in its mother's womb? Probably not. Does it know where it is? Probably not. Certainly not in any conscious way. Yet it is there, in the womb, asserting its existence. In that pre-partum existence, the fetus is coping – on its path to becoming a viable human being.

Do we, post-partum humans, know that we live in some sort of external womb? Probably not. We do live in the confines of that external womb. I'll call it Social Space. We may not be aware of it, but: *We live in, and through, and by the actions of Social Space.*

We are barely aware of the actual character of that Social Space, at least not consciously. We are almost replicating our pre-partum selves, of having only the vaguest awareness of, let alone understanding of, where we are. But now we exercise our ignorance with infinitely more sophistication than our pre-partum ancestors. We have consciousness. We have highly developed intellect. We have formal and informal education that inducts us into Social Space. With these tools we cope, as I emphasized in my recent book, *Immediacy: Our Ways of Coping in Everyday Life.* But beyond that it is high time we recognize that we live within Social Space that has a character and, yes, a nature of its own – which (along with our genetic make-up) shapes much of human life. This is the challenge we need to address. In the following pages I tackle it by trying to contribute some understanding about the nature of Social Space.

My approach to understanding Social Space is perhaps not so different from what physicists mean when they say that nature is best understood if we think of it as made up of *fields* – and that the mission of science is to understand such *fields,* their component parts and their basic characteristics. To achieve that understanding scientists often make use of "constructs"

– such as Gravitation and Relativity in physics, Valence and the Periodic Table in chemistry, and Chromosomes and DNA in biological genetics. I am going to investigate Social Space in that spirit. To do so I shall borrow quite a lot of illustrative material from my *Immediacy* book. But in the present book I do so from a very different perspective. There, I focused on the individual's everyday coping behavior (which is the subtitle of the *Immediacy* book). Here, in contrast, I focus on finding a way to understand Social Space by developing some constructs about Social Space. In the following pages I'll have us explore these four constructs: *Hidden Space; Closed Space; Transcended Space; Meaningful Space.* Although they are based on past observations, they can yield a sense of grounding in the present and, perhaps, in the future.

Hidden Space includes a "Second Path" that deals with ordinarily "Unmentionable" items in personal and societal discourse.

Closed Space includes "Closed Moral Systems" that offer complete moral systems -- guides of how life is to be lived -- but can exclude alternative moralities.

Transcended Space includes "Access to the Ultimate," claiming to bring it into the present, here and now.

Meaningful Space includes creating "Meaning" from the concrescence – a coming together and forming a new entity -- of disparate and distant items.

Here, to illustrate the powerful bearing of these constructs on actual social circumstances and events, is a brief sketch applying them to genocides.

These genocides happened during the 20h century. What do they have in common?

Jews by Germans!

Armenians by Turks!

Fellow-Cambodians — the intellectuals, the educated, the non-Communists — by Khmer Rouge Cambodians!

Tutsis by Hutus in Rwanda!

Non-Arabs in Darfur by the Janjaweed!

In each case, in the behavior of individual perpetrators, a Second Path prevailed. Former relationships to the victims — even intimate family relationships that comprised the First Path — were now discounted. An entirely different self came out into the open — based on activating previous Unmentionables — allowing no qualms about killing and maiming the identified enemy.

In each case, the process of genocide operated in the confines of a Closed Moral World, a Local Moral System where a special "morality" prevailed. It justified the mass killing, torture, and mutilations on supposedly high moral grounds. The deeds were not merely justified; they assumed the highest priority. They were believed to be essential. Other moral considerations, those outside the Local Moral Universe that prevailed at the time, were disavowed: irrelevant because a firm wall against them was in place.

In each case, a particular population was targeted as the Ultimate enemy. This "enemy" population was regarded as a supreme and immediate threat — a malignancy that could be, that must be eliminated. To achieve that goal — elimination of the Ultimate threat — individual actions were seen to contribute mightily. Individuals Transcended their small worlds by participating in the grand cause of targeting the Ultimate enemy.

In each case, distinctive Links entered into and became guests in people's present outlook. These harvested hatreds and antipathies from many and varied outside sources. It coalesced them into a mind-set that highlighted new Meaning about what was supposedly important in their life. This readily supported a murderous course of action against the "enemies."

This is a very brief, truncated way of suggesting that the four attributes of Social Space apply to real life, to things that really did, and still do happen.

In this book I am not going further into a detailed study of genocides. (I did so in two previous books, *Ordinary People and Extraordinary Evil* and *Confronting Evil*.) Instead, I'll be concentrating on refining the constructs about Social Space.

Hidden Space:

The Second Path Phenomenon

I. The thesis

140 years ago the English banker-and-scholar Walter Bagehot drew attention to "The Cake of Custom" – the beliefs, values, and institutionalized social preferences that prevail in a society at a particular period. In more modern language, one might call it the prevailing culture, with its expression of large societal patterns, such as democratic government. It also included personal behavior, such as one's preferences and activities in everyday living. It drew attention to how societies differ, based on their prevailing customs. And finally, it also drew interest to how change might take place – namely, in "shattering the cake of custom" by scholars who followed Bagehot's insights.

In the following pages I shall focus on what one might indelicately call the soft underbelly of a society's prevailing cake of customs. I'll do so by pointing to a particular feature of the cake of custom within the Social Space in which we live. Namely, openly expressed customs may not be the whole story of how we humans operate. That beneath the open, public expression of a culture's content – what I call The First Path – there can exist a hidden content, made up of current Unmentionables – what I call The Second Path. Despite being Unmentionable, that hidden content may be very much alive, even though, at a particular time, it may not be recognized or expressed openly. Yet in its hidden form it may continue to grow, sometimes in grotesquely extreme ways, precisely because it is not publicly acknowledged, accountable, and controlled. This creates the possibility that entirely discredited culture content may be available for activation at any time in the future – as the recent American presidential election seemed to indicate. And still another possibility is that some of our noblest aspirations can exist in a disabled, Unmentionable state.

II. Elaboration

My first clue that Social Space can contain a Hidden Space that nurtures Unmentionables came when I learned of the suicide of a number of Holocaust survivors who became highly successful writers. Among these were Primo Levi, Jerzy Kosinski, Tadeusz Borowski, Paul Celan, Jean Amery, and Bruno Bettelheim. I came to call their route to suicide a Second Path, in contrast to their First Path, their public persona as successful writers.

I shall also illustrate the Second Path phenomenon from the career of Walter Cronkite, the hurdles confronting many African-Americans, human sexuality, career Army officers, anti-Semitism in Nazi era Germany, and the moral dilemmas of two American presidents.
These bring out that Hidden Space can be a storage site of wisdom and noble aspirations, as well as a storage site of malignant and destructive potentials. In short, Hidden Space is not inherently evil or good. Merely, that it can be a component part of human Social Space. We need to understand how it works, not only to understand the current state of a society, but its potential for change and transformation.

First, the case of the Holocaust survivors who became highly successful writers, and committed suicide: These acclaimed writers had evidently found ways to lead meaningful and productive lives after surviving the horrors of the Holocaust. Yet eventually, after apparently successful, productive, rewarding and meaningful lives, they each committed suicide. The best known of these survivors was Primo Levi.

After surviving the Auschwitz concentration camp, Primo Levi briefly resumed his career as a chemist. But he soon turned to writing – and what a writer he became! He wrote about his experiences in the concentration camp. He was not a survivor who wallowed in suffering, who reiterated the horror of the horrors. He wrote as a participant and as a scientist who observed and reflected. He shared the poignancy of specific events and transcending insights that went beyond the individual events. He showed us the unique and the universal. He created balance between acknowledging the life-denying horrors and asserting life-affirming human dignity amid the horrors. His discernment seemed to rise above the seductions of evil.

Beyond his writings about Auschwitz, Primo Levi turned to topics that had little to do with the woes of human existence and much to do with celebrating life. He wrote of the joys to be discovered in nature and the inner world of science. In both, his fine-tuned spirituality softened the harsh impersonality of scientific reasoning. It seemed that Levi had found a way to celebrate the vibrancy of life. He had discovered for himself – and shared with those of us who read his writings – fresh ways to enjoy and celebrate membership in the human community. He did so through the healthy process of becoming a creative and active contributor to that community's zest for life. He accomplished all this by living in a magnificent First Path – where publicly and exuberantly, his own embrace of life was on display.

Yet this man committed suicide. And he was not alone. As I began to investigate it became disconcertingly clear that a number of Holocaust survivors who had become highly successful people committed suicide. What was going on? Perhaps, as my friend, the writer Henryk Grynberg states, these individuals had not truly "survived" the horrors. To be sure, they survived physically. But emotionally and psychically, they had not survived. Their early pain remained. The life-negations remained with them. They could never cleanse themselves of the poison planted in their souls.

I suggest that, in addition, within these individuals there actually was an internal process of escalating survivor guilt. It happened despite, and perhaps because of, their outward successes. Their subconscious sense of vulnerability, fear and terror, as well as guilt for having survived was never resolved, but actually kept on growing. This subterranean Second Path had a life of its own. Over time that Second Path became so engorged that it eventually erupted, dominating the individual's life, and found expression in the final act of despair, suicide.

A digression: Sigmund Freud saw the Unconscious as being part of one's personality that is largely hidden from conscious awareness. In Freud's view it is usually the result of early life experiences. The task of psychoanalysis, Freud said, is to retrace and rediscover these early, damaging experiences. I suggest that the second part of this formulation needs to be amended.

I am suggesting that there is also a Subconscious — the hidden part of one's personality — that may be *fed continually from one's ongoing life*. It is made up of items that are currently disagreeable, frightening, and Unmentionable. As part of our daily lives, we are continually shunting new awareness into a hidden niche — the Subconscious — because we perceive them as unacceptable and dangerous to ourselves. In the case of the Holocaust survivors who became successful, it is surely an error to assume that all factors in their post-Holocaust lives were comfortable, cozy, and satisfying. Instead, being nuanced and sensitive people, they could perceive many fearsome elements in their present lives. It is conceivable that their survivor guilt actually kept on growing while worldly success emphasized their increasing feeling of accountability to those who did not survive. Were their post-Holocaust successes — the awards they were receiving, their financial affluence — were these telling them that they were dancing on the graves of their loved ones? Was each award, each new acclaim for their writings, each "success," regarded as more failure? As their success increased so may their sense of dissonant linkage to those who were left to die, increasing their stored anguish and fragility.

A Primo Levi biographer, Myriam Anissimor, documents his Second Path to suicide.[1] She writes, "Forty years after his return (from Auschwitz) Levi was writing in torment about the fact that he had survived when most of his comrades had died…." She relates that a few days before his death in 1987, Levi telephoned the Chief Rabbi of Rome, saying, "I don't know how to go on. I can't stand this life any longer."[2] Two months before, he had written to a friend that what he was now experiencing was worse than

Auschwitz.[3] (I would ask: What was worse than Auschwitz? Had he won another award?)

There were other factors in Levi's life that augmented his assertive Second Path. He had suffered from depression and had been on anti-depressant medication. But after a difficult prostate surgery in March 1987, he had stopped taking the medication, surely adding to the fragility of his condition – amounting to his Second Path prevailing over his First Path, and dominating his social space.

Fragility – a balancing act between a First and Second Path – is not unique to survivors of horrors. It can also exist in the career of highly successful persons, where we least expect it. John Adams, Winston Churchill, Albert Einstein; their private lives suggest that, even at the height of their successful careers – their public First Paths – they acutely felt many hurts they had to absorb within themselves. To my knowledge, Einstein did not die a happy man.

I am reminded of a televised interview with Walter Cronkite, the retired television news anchorman.[4] During his tenure as the premier CBS news anchorman he was by far the most respected newscaster. For about two decades millions of viewers routinely turned on their television to receive news whose reliability they felt they could trust, because it was delivered by a man they trusted. To say that Walter Cronkite was respected is an understatement. For millions of people he was and still is deeply revered, long after his retirement and death.

Yet in the interview, conducted during his eightieth year, Cronkite expressed open hurt about being slighted by the television network he had served so long. Nowadays, he said, they did not invite him to their receptions and parties. He was made to feel unwelcome when he visited the newsroom where he used to work. This revered man expressed discomfort that is truly astounding. Here was a man who had earned the highest respect from millions of people. Yet he now felt hurt when a few people – people of infinitely less accomplishment than his – did not show him respect. How could such a man – a man of such poise, sobriety, and strength – be so vulnerable? What is it in his social space that produced this result?

As a rule, highly respected people do not express their fears and vulnerabilities in public. Not, at least, during their tenure in highly esteemed roles, when protective walls insulate the occupant from confronting their vulnerabilities. In the case of the interview with Mr. Cronkite we saw him during his retirement from the esteemed role. He was no longer insulated by a protective wall. Furthermore, the interview was conducted by a tabloid-type of program – the sort of program Cronkite would have shunned during this tenure as esteemed journalist. In the course of the interview his emotional vulnerability was deliberately milked. His discomfort was exploited. The interview claimed to show the "human side" of this noble man while, in fact, stripping him of his humanity by displaying to all of us that he, too, had a fearful inner side. At the age of eighty he was more vulnerable than ever. In his current social space, his Second Path lay exposed.

Look at the social space occupied by an adult in our society. Compared to a child, it contains diminished freedom to admit weakness, to express fears and uncertainties. These, when they do occur, may be safeguarded in a subconscious vault, a Second Path. But they can unexpectedly erupt. In which sort of social space are they likely to erupt? Or, stored safely? Or, routinely dissipated and not stored at all? I do not have good answers. But a safe guess is that leaders and persons of high status may be especially constrained against admitting weakness, and therefore prone to cultivating a Second Path.

In former times, within the traditional one-career family the spouse, usually the wife, sometimes served as the receptacle for the male careerist's work-related Unmentionables. He might bring home and there express the frustrations, fears and rage he experienced in the course of his work. Onto his wife he could safely dump these career negatives without worry that they would be communicated to his career peers. It was safe to do so. (It was safe for the male careerist, but not so safe for the wife when the husband might come home in a state of fury.) With the advent of two-career families this safety valve has largely disappeared. The wife is no longer shut off from the world of work contacts. And she has Unmentionable work frustrations of her own that require attention outside the work context. There is rarely room for two sets of career frustrations to be vented and receive nurturing. Unmentionables can remain dangerously repressed, awaiting explosive eruption or, at least, a change of spouse who "really understands you."

Return to the Freudian notion of the Unconscious, supposedly based on the individual's early life experiences, and never resolved, and raising their ugly head occasionally. The Unconscious can be aroused – usually in destructive ways – by current events in the individual's life, but basically made up of the long-buried experiences. How realistic is this? Can one reduce the discomfort of the eighty-year-old Walter Cronkite to unresolved early childhood experiences that remained buried inside? Surely this is stretching credulity, and misunderstanding of Mr. Cronkite's social space.

By contrast, consider that in the ongoing life of adults a Subconscious can be created and continually nurtured. The individual's present life, the here and now, can contain elements that are continually shunted aside to a place hidden from the individual's public posture – into what I call the Second Path. It can contain items of discomfort that an apparently confident individual would be loath to admit, even to oneself. This discomfort may not be a childhood discomfort, as the Freudians might picture it, but an entirely adult discomfort, based on real – but Unmentionable – interpretations of circumstances in the individual's present life. In the case of Walter Cronkite, the insults to his person were perpetrated after the zenith of his career. That is when there was vulnerability. The dagger hit its mark. It had spotted a current weakness.

What is unusual about the Walter Cronkite case is that the discomfort's impact was revealed in full public view. Ordinarily such discomfort is carefully hidden. It is shunted into a siding where neither the public nor the self is allowed to be fully aware of what is happening. Only in dreams does one occasionally dare to confront such discomfort. In dreams, too, it tends to arrive in veiled forms that make it difficult to understand its source and intrusion into our current ways of living.

As Freud taught many of us, dreams are often actively displayed versions of the Unconscious. One might call it a display of the Second Path within a social space. When we read the biblical story of Jacob wrestling with God's representative during the night, we are shown the unsettling restlessness that can get the upper hand during the night. The theologian Walter Bruegeman tells us that we may experience night's limitless, wondrous side as well as its unconstrained, fearsome side.[5] What Bruegeman calls "nighttime work" – with its profound wrestling with one's conscience, its occasional eruption of total terror – contrasts with "daytime work," where humans may seem to have control over their destiny. "During the day [Jacob] is able to manage and able to take initiative. But at night, as for all of us, Jacob turns out to be vulnerable, and things rush powerfully beyond his control. His night is peopled by those uninvited and unwelcome in his life. But they are the very ones with whom he has to come to terms, if he is to go home peaceably."[6] In dreams, the Second Path is openly at work. It is in full view.

Speaking of the Second Path being in full view, perhaps the most pitiful current examples exist among mentally impaired individuals who are outside the mental illness support system. Large long-term psychiatric hospitals have been closed, sending many patients out into the community, in the hope that medications and community support will take care of their needs. Instead, we find many severely ill individuals trapped without family or other community support, without their needed medication, living on the street, engaged in petty crime that lands them in prisons that are entirely unsuited to treating mental patients. There, in the prison, their Second Path, filled with their fears, their phobias, their hallucinations – can be on full display in the form of crude ways of acting out. These are sometimes met with brutal punishment instead of medical treatment. The medically impaired lack a First Path that might hide their illness. Instead, the raw presence of their Second Path can elicit ever more brutal responses from prison personnel, who operate under the mandate of prisons: to punish, to secure order, to protect society against individuals under their control.

Another manifestation of an active Second Path showed up in relations between blacks and whites in America as recently as the 1990s. At that time Glenn Loury, a distinguished black economist, wrote: "Arguably the most race-obsessed people in America today are not the Southern rednecks but rather the well-educated and prosperous black elites.[7]

This bears out my own impressions – unscientifically gathered, but convincing to me – that some blacks who, by general American standards, are highly successful, seem to be the most despairing. These are persons who in their personal careers and their standard of living in both economic and educational terms are highly successful. Yet they seem to feel fiercely that they are being denied their full and rightful place by the white race – a race with whose members they now have the closest contact.

Loury's explanation is that such members of the black middle class are finally having a chance to express themselves and be heard by their former oppressors – who are now "not strangers, but….neighbors and coworkers.. For the first time, they engage their oppressors in moral discourse as political equals." It gives such blacks "a greater opportunity to express the racial injustices they still feel."

This is surely plausible. But it does not seem to account for the high level of race obsession – "the racial injustice they still feel"—among the "advantaged" blacks that Loury describes. It does not appear to account for the seemingly high level of feeling bereft experienced and expressed by at least some of these persons. It seems to me that their anguish refers not merely to those blacks who are still disadvantaged, who live in poverty and high crime districts in the cities, and who (in Loury's words) make up a disproportionately large share of the underclass. It does not seem to account for their memory of past horrors historically inflicted on blacks.

On the contrary, they seem to be speaking of their own situation, of their own lives, of here and now, where they appear to be doing so well. How can this be?

For many of these successful blacks, the route to economic success has surely been beset by unanticipated and unjustified hurdles. The successful black professional – the physician, the lawyer, the college professor – has had to answer the spoken or unspoken query: Are you an affirmative action beneficiary, without "real" credentials for your job? Such cruel and usually unfounded denigrations are probably part of the burden borne by many a black professional. Such biases ignore the likelihood that an individual who reaches a high-level occupation despite a disadvantaged background may thereby demonstrate extraordinary initiative, hard work, and much practical intelligence. The supposed affirmative action beneficiary may still operate under the burden of forever having to prove that one really deserves to be where one is at this time.

The pattern of denigrating the affirmative-action beneficiary ignores another variant of this phenomenon: The struggle of traditionally disadvantaged categories of individuals – women and Jews, as well as blacks and each wave of new immigrants. To achieve social and economic success, these persons had to perform at far higher levels than individuals born of high status, who were habitually given preferential treatment for admission to elite universities and occupations.

I have cited just one factor, the accusation of being an affirmative-action product, in the memory of many a black person who has struggled to achieve the American dream. Surely, there are many more items to which a black individual can be acutely sensitive. I am reminded of an accomplished black lawyer whose career struggles were described in a biography written by his (white) Harvard University roommate.[8] The book describes his beginnings in a housing project. He excelled in school, went on to Harvard undergraduate school through a scholarship, then on to Harvard Law School, then to a prominent law firm. He suddenly resigned from the law firm and brought a lawsuit against that firm – probably ensuring his elimination from any future employment by a mainstream law firm – in response to perceived racial discrimination against him. To an outsider, this man's career, until his resignation from he law firm, appears to be a grand success story. But this does not do justice to what really happened.

The biography highlights a Second Path in his life, which eventually exploded into the open. The lawyer had attempted to play by America's rules, from his early childhood on into his adulthood: Hard work, avoid drugs or any deviant subculture temptations and, along the way, avoid responding to racial slurs that came his way many a time – including seeing

10

a Harvard friend receive a note deploring that friend's "associating with a nigger." His awareness of racism became increasingly impossible to bear in silence. He perceived that this law firm discriminated against him because of his race, even when it was ever so subtle, and blocked his life aspirations. He saw his lawsuit "as the culmination of all his past frustrations…related to race"[9] and seeing his treatment by the firm "as disrespecting his entire life's mission to overcome disadvantage."[10]

The book gives a glimpse of the other side as well, namely the jaundiced view about affirmative action beneficiaries. A member of the law firm is cited as saying that the above-mentioned black lawyer "was probably an affirmative action hire who just did not work out."[11]

It seems that the memory of racial struggles in the course of a career can attain a dormant life – paralleling the life of the Holocaust survivor's painful experiences – where the pain is not only not extinguished, once and for all, but may actually be fed even while an individual is allegedly successful in everyday life. That dormant Second Path is the cumulative haven of painful Unmentionables that won't go away, that may even continue to be fed in one's current life, which may eventually force themselves upon the individual's public self.

Another example of a Second Path – a cumulative haven for Unmentionables that eventually forces itself into the forefront of the individual's life – is the career life of demons of Glenda Jackson, a famous British actress. She was a highly acclaimed actress, then became a Member of Parliament after she abruptly left her acting career. She has been described as follows: "Jackson, who has two Best Actress Oscars, and was a 1972 Emmy winner…walked away from movie celebrity in 1992…During a twenty-seven-year acting career, she suffered from extreme stage fright; she told *The Guardian* newspaper that 'the longer I carried on, the greater the fear became.'" [12] (As I write this, in 2016, she has returned to acting on stage.)

Stage fright is fairly common among even highly accomplished actors. The Unmentionable called stage fright typically contains an assortment of conflicting items – fear of the audience before stepping onto the stage and embracing the audience; love for the audience in combination with dread of what the audience can do to your personal identity; the realization that you are baring your innermost soul to the audience while despising yourself for being so naked, but not being able to live without it. Such Unmentionables exist in symbiosis with the actor's public performance, one's First Path. Once fully and explicitly acknowledged – as did Glenda Jackson – the actor could no longer continue to act.

Luciano Pavarotti, perhaps the greatest modern tenor, stated that before every performance he is in a state of total terror. That terror ends when he steps on stage. Each successful venture onto the stage is a victory over stage fright, over self-doubt and weakness, over cold terror. It boils down to this: the Unmentionables of stage fright enable performers to do things they dread but love beyond all else. In their state of partial acknowledgement, the stage fright Unmentionables becomes an addiction. One dreads it and one needs it.

Stated differently, the phenomenon of stage fright is an enactment of warfare between an individual's First and Second Paths. It amounts to awareness of the conjoint existence of both Paths in an individual's Social Space and when, for once, neither of its components is silent. The act of overcoming stage fright is an occasion of victory of the First Path. But the victory is temporary. Just before the next public performance, if we are to believe Pavarotti, the battle will have to be fought again.

Let me consider another example of an individual's internal warfare between the First and Second Paths. It comes to us from Freud drawing attention to the untamed sexuality that was largely covered up in polite Viennese society of his time. His thesis was that many neurotic illnesses had their roots in early childhood sexual experiences that were repressed, but surfaced occasionally in the form of socially inappropriate and neurotic behavior.

I agree with Freud's disclosure of sex-related neuroses. But I disagree with his explanation – that most neuroses were due to early childhood experiences. I suggest that he was depicting ongoing warfare between the First and Second Paths within an individual's Social Space.

Freud presented us with an awareness of pervasive sexuality that is diffused and sublimated in many ways. In most societies sexuality is tamed by being funneled into approved social roles, such as marital roles and, more contemporarily, into long-lasting relationships. In our society, pervasive sexuality is buttressed through an elaborate belief system that unrestrained sexuality is largely attributable to raging hormones during youth that, sooner or later, are supposedly outgrown as the individual enters into "responsible" adult social roles. There sexuality is socially controlled and harnessed for the procreation and care of the next generation and sublimated in the decorum governing dealings among adults. Roughly speaking, we may call this sexuality in the First Path. It is our culture's Mentionable sexuality.

Now, let us consider sexuality in the Second Path, where Unmentionables play a part. Let us realize, first of all, that human sexuality is relatively permanent, whatever form it takes. Throughout the individual's life, there is ongoing input to and output from one's sexuality. This comes not only from biology (namely, hormones) but also from, and to, the social environment, whose culture can be pervaded by sexual themes.

In the course of daily life there are many sexually tinged transactions among daily activities. There are interactions between individuals who are potential sexual partners. There is exposure to a culture, notably American marketing culture, where sexuality is pervasively used to promote commerce in goods and services. Here sex is often used as a catalyst for non-sexual activities, such as selling cars, toothpaste, furniture. In short, sex in many a subtle form is used as an economic commodity. All this cannot fail to link up with the individual's sexual reservoir – sexual awareness and sexual responsiveness – and both aware and unacknowledged acceptance of sexual relevance to many ongoing activities.

Given the existing societal rules about appropriate expression of sexuality, there is also an ongoing process of covering up socially inappropriate sexual input. After all, it is potentially disruptive to the individual's existing social relationships and responsibilities. Yet the culturally supported sexual titillations continue, and so do the personal cover-ups.

Concerning cover-ups, I am reminded of Picasso's early erotic paintings that have thus far (as I write these words) been prevented from being shown in the United States. These paintings may overdo their focus on sexuality. But it seems clear that this is not salacious pornography. Rather, these paintings exuberantly celebrate sex as a portal to life itself. Picasso was intoxicated with life, and focus on sexuality was, in his youth and throughout his life, a core celebration of life – at least, that is my view.

In America there is an ongoing build-up of sexual dissonance, of culturally sponsored sexual schizophrenia, an ongoing input of sexual expression that is both socially sponsored and induced and, at the same time, defined as inappropriate if expressed too openly. Certainly the early Picasso paintings were far too explicit an expression of sexuality for American comfort. The sex input can often be stored, and rechanneled, relatively safely. But it may also accumulate in a way that shows up precisely in the form of neuroses and dysfunctional behavior that Freud so accurately noted. I would call it the occasional intrusion of the Second Path – one's sexual Unmentionables – into the Social Space we call our everyday life. I differ from Freud, let me repeat, in emphasizing that sexual experiences defined as inappropriate can be both generated and continually enhanced in adulthood. It can happen in the course of regular life as offered in our society.

In a larger sense, the so-called untamed sexuality of youth as well as life-long sexuality of human adults may well have its evolutionary roots in an underlying biological-genetic reality that has persisted over eons and has left an imprint on how we lead our lives. After our birth two contrasting processes appear to operate. Namely, alongside the development of our individuation – in the form of a new and separate life, particularly after childhood, when we are defined as full-fledged, separate, and independent creatures – there remains a quest for bonding that sees comfort and security through closeness and intimacy with another human being. We humans lead individual lives, but we are not self-sufficient creatures. The biological imperative seems to be that we have inherited a fundamental duality: a quest for separation and a quest for fusion. Perhaps the dual paths in our personal lives are a way of coping with that dual inheritance – and with its discordant messages and yearnings – usually stored in a Second Path's separation from a First Path.

Awareness of Unmentionables and a Second Path takes me back to my tour of duty in the U. S. Army in the 1950s. I was an enlisted man, assigned to an Administrative unit in the army's Infantry School at Ft. Benning, Georgia. That Infantry School was an advanced training center – more like a university – where officials took refresher courses at a high level of sophistication, critical to their careers in the infantry. My job included keeping records on the performance of Army officers who were taking courses. It was somewhat incongruous. I, a lowly enlisted man (along with several other enlisted men) serving as a clerk, was keeping records on officers who ranged in rank all the way up to general.

The officers were individuals who had made service in the army their professional career. Many of them attained senior positions following service in a variety of military campaigns. Occasionally some of them visited the office where the records were kept and inquired about their grades.

It struck me that these individuals – who often had distinguished career achievements behind them and were, even now, holding down highly regarded positions – were exceedingly fearful about their grades. It seemed that anything less than very high scores on the tests was totally crushing to them. They appeared apprehensive, anxious, worried. These were senior officers in the Army. They were men of high accomplishment who ordinarily had considerable confidence, sophistication and poise. Yet here all their confidence, sophistication, and poise seemed to desert them. They acted as though their entire careers were in jeopardy.

As I now understand it, there may have been real justification for these officers' apprehensiveness. Promotion to the next rank or getting a coveted new assignment might indeed be affected by their test scores. But at the time it seemed to me that these men were terribly and inordinately scared; that they were elevating that molehill of their performance into a major mountain.

As I now see it the officers' increasing confidence, sophistication and poise, nurtured and developed over the years of a successful career, might be just one dimension of the Social Space permeating their lives. Perhaps alongside it there might also have been a parallel, though subterranean, growth of apprehension and uncertainty. This second dimension – this Second Path – the obverse of their publicly visible career manifestations – was ordinarily dormant and hidden. But on occasion it could erupt into the open.

Stated differently, as the Army officers advanced in their careers they were playing for ever-higher stakes. They engaged in ever-more responsible and rewarding endeavors. But career opportunities became more limited. After all, the career pyramid gets very narrow at the top. There is only one Chief of the Army. In any race for that coveted top spot there are bound to be losers. In deciding who will get to occupy the very few positions at or near the top, some – the majority of those eligible – are going to be left out. It may well be the ones with a slightly lower score on a test – even in a minor course. It may give those above you, who will make the decision about your fate, a basis for deciding among competing candidates, all of whom may be fully qualified for advancement!

Let us say there are ten fully qualified candidates for one position. Each candidate has distinguished and successful career accomplishments. Then a way must be found to eliminate nine individuals. It is quite possible, then, that one candidate's "B" grade on a course, when others made an "A" grade, might eliminate that candidate. The issue is not that the "B" grade is, in itself, an indicator of low professional competence. It is simply a tool by which military superiors might eliminate a person from consideration. They may use quite trivial criteria to make the selection when, in fact, every one of the ten candidates is fully qualified to fill the opening. The decision-makers are not apt to admit this openly. Instead, they might say that, in one's personal judgment, a particular candidate really stands out.

In short, there can be a real basis for the seeming over-emphasis on the importance of a grade on a test. It really can knock individuals out of the running for the grand prize, the pinnacle of a professional career. The officers' fears could be fully justified.

I am speculating that the pinnacle of one's career – what you have striven for, the next step you can almost taste – would be for naught if you failed to get that final promotion. Might an entire career be diminished if you failed to reach that final goal? Here, if true, is a powerful assortment of Unmentionable uncertainties, yearnings, and fears! To forestall a career derailment and validate what one has been struggling to achieve for such a long time, one absolutely must reach the next higher rung on the ladder. Most importantly, reaching that rung could be derailed by even the most minor missteps, such as middling grade on a minor refresher course.

Here is a hypothesis: On the surface, it seems that the Army officers' career evolution was necessarily accompanied by more confidence, sophistication, and poise. But its obverse – the uncertainties, the fear of failure and missteps – might grow alongside the public posture. These attributes might also keep pace with the career's evolution, growing apace with it. They are not likely to be the same sorts of fears that the young military officer experienced at the beginning of that career. Instead, these fears are appropriate to the stage of the career in which an officer finds oneself. They have grown alongside the career's evolution; they are career-stage specific. But, if anything, they may be more terrifying than the terrors in the early stages of the career. There is now far greater sophistication about the pitfalls and dangers to one's reputation and one's future. Altogether, these Unmentionables constitute a Second Path in one's career – a component part of one's Social Space.

A word of caution: Thus far I have described patterns of an intrusive Second Path that seem to afflict a least some individuals. I do not claim that this is bound to happen to every human being in the various categories I have been describing. Not every Holocaust survivor is afflicted with pain that escalates to the point of eventual suicide, or even being seriously temped to commit suicide. Not every black, middle-class American is afflicted with ever-expanding, though subterranean, racist disenchantment. Not every adult is afflicted with sexually derived neuroses whose sources are adult, rather than childhood experiences. Not every senior military officer is burdened with escalating fears and uncertainty. In short, I do not know how prevalent is an intrusive Second Path. Yet when it does occur, it constitutes a potentially explosive compound that may suddenly erupt and intrude into the life of the individual, transforming it drastically by dominating one's Social Space.

Furthermore, Unmentionable components of the Second Path may not be unhealthy or pathological. To be sure they are made up of items the social space deems inappropriate for bringing out into the open. Hence these items are shunted into a silent siding, perhaps temporarily, perhaps permanently. Yet these shunted Unmentionables – stored in a Second Path – may be the most honest, the most moral, the healthiest responses to the reality that currently exists.

General George Lee Butler comes to mind. Since his retirement from the U.S. Air Force he has been a leading organizer of an effort to fully eliminate nuclear weapons on our planet.[13] Using his personal visibility, his wide circle of social contacts, his considerable energy and passion, he assembled support from leading figures in many countries.

Before his retirement General Butler commanded America's nuclear weapons. Given an order by the president, General Butler would have been in charge of dropping nuclear bombs onto any designated enemy. While he was the general in charge of the nuclear forces, he obviously could not advocate, publicly or privately, the elimination of these weapons. Perhaps he could not even think these thoughts. But surely before his retirement he held these views, somewhere, somehow, about the terrible dangers, inherent immorality, and uselessness of these weapons for promoting a humane world. In his pre-retirement position these views were Unmentionable. The views had to be kept in silent storage while he commanded America's nuclear weapons. After leaving his post in the military service (in the 1990s), he became free to tell us:

"We continue to espouse (nuclear) deterrence as if it were now an infallible panacea. And worse, others are listening, have converted to our theology, are building their [nuclear] arsenals, are poised to rekindle the nuclear arms race – and reawaken the specter of nuclear war...we have won...the opportunity to reset mankind's moral compass, to renew belief in a world free from fear and deprivation, to win global affirmation for the sanctity of life, the right of liberty and the opportunity to pursue a joyous existence."[14]

In a similar vein, one is reminded of Dwight Eisenhower's warnings against this country's "military industrial complex" as he was about to leave office as president of the United States. He had a highly distinguished career as military officer that culminated in the presidency of the United States. Both careers surely uniquely qualified him to be aware of the "military industrial complex." It is not known why he did not make his warning statement during his time in high office. What we do know is that he made the statement – the only one of its kind by him, as far as I now – only as he was leaving office as president. Presumably he believed he was in no position to voice these views during his career in high office. One can only speculate that had he made the warning statement during his time in office, it might have carried greater weight, and produced far more impact. I speculate again, we are left with a glimpse of his Unmentionables – that shunted Second Path -– that gave him moral anguish while he occupied, in turn, the highest military and the highest civilian offices of his country.

Another president, Lyndon Johnson, was eventually run out of office due to the increasing unpopularity of America's involvement in the Vietnam War. He vehemently defended America's role in that war. While he was personally blamed for escalating that conflict. He was depicted as the personification of a wicked course of action. Day after day demonstrators attacked him for sending hundreds of thousands of American troops into a war that seemed not only unwinnable but increasingly unjustified -– on pragmatic, political, as well as moral grounds. The outcry against Johnson reached such giant proportions that he was obliged to turn away from running for a second term as president.

Yet years later the records reveal that Johnson had grave misgivings about the Vietnam War, even while he was publicly defending it. Indeed he actually shared the views of his critics – that the Vietnam War was not worth fighting and that it was morally indefensible. He held these views even before he entered into the process of escalating the number of American troops he was sending into that war. In his public pronouncements Johnson continued to strongly defend America's involvement. In his public actions he increased America's participation in that war.

Yet in his private world, in the Unmentionables of his Second Path, he was totally appalled by the war and America's participation in it. (As I write these words I remember Rudolf Hoess, the commander of the Auschwitz concentration camp, saying that he was appalled by some of the brutality at Auschwitz, WHILE HE WAS IN CHARGE OF THAT CAMP. I wrote about it – and tried to explain it -- in my book, "Ordinary People and Extraordinary Evil.") While publicly Johnson appeared to be self-assured and unflinching in his support of the war, he confided to his friend, Senator Richard Russell, the chairman of the Senate Armed Services Committee, "We're in the quicksand up to our neck, and I just don't know what the hell to do about it."[15] This was in May 1964, before the largest build-up of American troops. That day, too, he told his national security advisor, McGeorge Bundy, "I don't think it's worth fighting for, and I don't think we can get out." Despite the increasing public outcry against the war, the president was even more afraid of the Congress – "they'd impeach a president, though, that would run out [and abandon the Vietnam War], wouldn't they?"[16] In that situation, says a commentator, "No president can be seen as vacillating. He had to be seen as prudent but also as a strong anti-Communist."[17]

Thanks to the tapes released by the LBJ Library, we have access to information about President Johnson's shunted Second Path, filled with Unmentionables. That Second Path was carefully shielded from the public, while its converse – the self-assured escalator of the war – grew in the public's eye. Yet the Second Path also grew, receiving input daily and becoming evermore stressful to its owner.

Dynamics of Unmentionables

From what you have just read, there is every indication that the Second Path is more than a safe storage place, a repository of items that are publicly Unmentionable -- deemed embarrassing, hurtful, or inappropriate. It turns out that within an individual's Social Space stored material can sometimes flow from one's Second Path into one's First Path. Ugly Unmentionables can then come into public view. Behind this event is the likelihood that the Second Path has internal dynamics of its own. It is not inert. This is what I want us to consider next.

First of all, let us bear in mind that the Second Path is likely to be made up of items from life experiences that have not been resolved, but are potentially available for active interplay with current life experiences. Here we may find seemingly incongruously linkages and interactions among supposedly separate events. For example, Time, as we usually think of it, may be disregarded: Something that happened long ago is assumed to be happening right now, and be on a par with matters that really are happening now, and be in interaction with them. [18]

Let us take an imaginary look at some elderly occupants of a nursing home. Here bewildering occasions from childhood may re-awaken and be linked to bewildering occasions in one's current geriatric existence in the nursing home since, in some ways, an individual my once again be treated as a child. Public routines, one's First Path in the nursing home, may be carried out against the not-so-subtle internal battles awakened by these two sets of bewildering occasions, each reinforcing the other. This happens even though one of the bewildering occasions occurred many years ago, and the other, although it is of recent origin, cannot be acknowledged if the person is to retain some dignity as a fully functioning adult. The two bewildering occasions may now form a mutually reinforcing system of alienation and disorientation from the nursing home in which the individual now resides, where two widely "separate" experiences are now experienced as one single event, occurring right now. Within the Second Path the two experiences have collapsed into one set of bewildering Unmentionables that dominate one's current Social Space.

What kind of "systemic" processes are apt to be at work within the individual's Social Space, where the Second Path spills over into the individual's First Path, the individual's publicly acknowledged life? The best approach may be through cybernetics, the science of self-regulating systems. It looks at systems entirely on the basis of internal dynamics.[19] Therefore, here are a few words about cybernetics. I shall begin with some rather theoretical statements about cybernetics, then apply these to our issues here.

Four kinds of cybernetics have been identified. One cybernetic is where equilibrium is maintained. Feedback processes, operating within the system, keep the system in balance by counteracting any drastic disturbance. A thermostat attached to a furnace is an example of such a feedback mechanism. When your home gets too hot, the thermostat shuts the furnace off. When your home gets too cold, the thermostat restarts the furnace. In each situation the feedback arrangement operates to keep the temperature in the house within a particular range. Here, cybernetics assures a stable equilibrium of the temperature in the house.

The second cybernetics promotes growth. Here, too, are feedback processes within a system, but they serve to keep the system growing. It does so by reinforcing each "deviation," allowing it to become cumulative and continue in one direction. Here is an example: Why did a particular city arise in a particular location in a Middle East desert? Perhaps a trading caravan had to stop because the axle on one of its wagons broke. It took more than a day to repair the axle. Hence arrangements had to be made to set up facilities for a more lengthy stay. This led to a search for water, perhaps even to digging a well. A search for food began, perhaps leading to discovery of relatively nutritious plant life in the vicinity. Some individuals found that they enjoyed gathering food much more than the frequent travel in the caravan. And so forth. In short, after an initial accidental event, one response led to another, each reinforcing the evolving pattern of the group's settling down and creating the conditions for permanent residence. It may have included eventually erecting a religious shrine in celebration of communal living. Technically speaking, each positive feedback led to another positive feedback, all pointing the way from the frequent-travel mode of living toward settling down and creating a settled community.

The third cybernetic is where the system is frozen into rigidity. It is not responsive at all. If there are feedback processes within the system, they serve only to inhibit responsiveness. The clinically dead are typical examples.

The fourth cybernetic (the opposite of the third) is where there is extreme responsiveness. There is response to each and every stimulus. In our life we cannot possibly react to every single stimulus that comes our way – not each day, not each hour, not each moment. If we did attempt to respond to each and every stimulus, we would surely be dead by the end of the day. In technical jargon, this leads to entropy, the system's dissolution. If there are feedback processes, they serve only to escalate responsiveness, until the system is destroyed through exhaustion and dissipation.

In terms of the individual's personality and functioning as an individual, the first cybernetic can promote equanimity. Here the Second Path handles un-confronted pains and discordant experiences in ways that ensure that they not spill over into the First Path. The various Unmentionables are so smoothly controlled that they are not likely to emerge in system-disrupting ways. They are safely shunted aside. Within the individual's Social Space the First and Second Path co-exist, with the First Path prevailing.

Similarly, in the second cybernetics, there are no system disruptions. Instead, the capability to handle pain and discordant experiences expands. In popular language, we talk about a person becoming increasingly "mature" enough to handle adversity, to "grow" to accept discordant elements without being destructively distraught. Unmentionables are acknowledged, but they are not allowed to interfere. Instead, they may be harnessed to promote growth.

In the third cybernetics, things change. Here is frozen rigidity. Here the system does not respond to stimuli at all. This was the case with the Musselman in concentration camps. These individuals walked around like zombies, entirely unresponsive to their environment. And, because of their unresponsiveness, destined to die very soon. They had given up on life. Here the Unmentionables – and with it the Second Path – are in total control. And the First Path, which allows for some accommodation to the real world, is destroyed. Since it results in death, the net result is similar to the previously mentioned suicide of survivors. But in this case death results because of passivity, through unresponsiveness to one's surroundings, whereas among the former, death results from excessive responsiveness to one's surroundings (from suddenly responding to stimuli they thought they had overcome long ago).

In short, the third cybernetic is very likely to destroy the Social Space of individual human beings – both their First and Second Paths – and their capacity to function. It opens the way to the fourth cybernetic, the process of total dissolution, where entropy prevails; where once existed a system of functioning Social Space – in the form of a human life – sheer randomness takes over. Organized life no longer exists. A once-vibrant Social Space is replaced by a void.

I suspect that the Holocaust survivors who became successful writers but ended their lives through suicide went through a period of "growth" (a second cybernetics) when their personality widened as they wrote about life-affirming matters. They seemed to have reached a way of leading a satisfying and rewarding life. This was evident in their First Path. But in their Second Path, concomitantly, there grew a second cybernetic version of very different attributes. The life-denying attributes expanded and mutually reinforced each other, fed by the very successes that marked their First Path's apparent health. Within their Second Path, each award, each new public acclaim reinforced self-doubt and a sense of betraying those who were no longer here to accept acclaim and success. The Unmentionables were in full ascendance. This finally erupted by transforming the second cybernetic into a fourth cybernetic pattern – of extreme responsiveness to issues the individual had carefully avoided until that moment – bringing with it the full destruction of self.

As this illustrates, the transformation of a Second Path's second cybernetic into a fourth cybernetic can be destructive to the individual's First Path and, on occasion, to life itself. The Second Path, instead of serving as a safety valve for the First Path – of storing items the First Path cannot handle – that Second Path now becomes a threatening force that may annihilate the First Path, once its content of Unmentionables gain control.

This raises new questions. When does such a disastrous transformation take place? When does the conflict between the First Path and Second Path make life untenable? When do Unmentionables become unbearable? Can a Social Space protect itself? At this point I do not have answers. I only have urgent questions which, I hope, will stimulate more thought and investigation. You, my dear reader, may want to join the effort.

A Postscript: Social Space in which a Second Path operates on a large scale.

Consider anti-Semitism in pre-Hitler Germany. Some anti-Semitism existed. But it was largely Unmentionable. It was a taboo topic in polite "modern" Germany. Jews considered themselves to be fully integrated into mainstream German life. They shunned public indication of differences from gentile Germans. Most of them accepted that they were Jews. But above all they regarded themselves as Germans. Being German, they believed, was their primary identity. Any public acknowledgement of Jewish "separateness" was Unmentionable – by Jews themselves and by the broader German public. I repeat, anti-Semitism, although sporadically appearing, was not a polite topic in mainstream, pre-Hitler German life. It was not only Unmentionable. Perhaps it was really absent?

Hitler's Germany shattered this myth. Unmentionable anti-Semitism was suddenly and fulsomely activated. So fulsomely, in fact, that it provided the grounding for a murderous campaign unmatched in human history.

Stated differently, the Second Path that had once safe guarded German Jews by keeping German anti-Semitism invisible, turned out to host anti-Semitism that was very much alive – but in a dormant state that made it seemed to have changed. In its dormant state it could actually grow, despite its invisibility. And because of its invisibility, broader "modernity's" controls were absent. Hence, Hitler was able to activate and cultivate a level of anti-Semitism of unspeakable brutality and horror. He was able to do so by converting dormant, Second Path anti-Semitism into murderous, First Path anti-Semitism.

A comparable phenomenon – of massive activation of dormant anti-Semitism – took place in France during the Dreyfus Affair, in the early part of the previous century. There, too, Jews had been highly assimilated into that nation's life, but were suddenly awakened to the reality of deep and widespread levels of anti-Semitism. It did not reach the level of Hitler-Germany's murderous expression of anti-Semitism, but it shared much of Germany's demonstration of activating dormant, Second Path anti-Semitism being converted into active, First Path anti-Semitism.

III. Assessment

Finally, what do the examples and illustrations I have ben describing tell us about Hidden Space as a characteristic of Social Space? What do they tell us about its distinctive contributions to the structure of Social Space, and the functioning of human life in Social Space? Here are some thoughts.

(1) Hidden Space provides a safety net against disruption of current, orderly operations and consensus. Whether you call it protecting the status quo or preserving tranquility or assuring predictability of communal life, this feature has consequences, whether or not your own values support it. In America, for example, we have the continuing separatist, anti-federal yearnings perpetuated, mostly in some southern states, that are not openly and publicly asserted, thus keeping "the union" intact. In contrast to efforts leading up to the Civil War, the current separatist yearnings are now largely hidden.

(2) Hidden Space provides opportunities to explore unpopular options. Of course this raises the issue of just how unpopular, how extreme, can "exploration" be before it endangers the existing societal balance and consensus? The exploration can range from personal daydreaming of engaging in Unmentionable behavior, to fictional literary and other artistic exploration of Unmentionables, to the popularity of pornography. All these may by-pass respectable

Mentionables. But they do so in a format that guarantees their institutionalized status as "deviant-but-permitted," guaranteeing that the existing orthodoxies remain intact, while permitting circumscribed exploration beyond the Mentionables.

(3) Hidden Space preserves options, even if they are currently unpopular, out of favor, perhaps even hated. In recent times we have heard that universities are coming to be increasingly focused on limiting their offerings to what is currently intellectually and popularly in fashion, to research that is fundable, and to preparing students for currently viable occupations. This is precisely the opposite of what universities exemplified – or were thought to exemplify – in the past. Namely, offering highly diverse content – be it popular or unpopular, practical or impractical. They championed intellectual open-ness within Social Space that was largely hidden from public scrutiny and control.

(4) Hidden Space enables partial exploration of options before they are fully activated and implanted in actual behavior. In a sense, all formal education – from pre-school and grade school through college and graduate school – is about learning options in life before one is actually inducted into adult enactments, of making choices using one's options. Although we speak of "public" education, in actuality education is partially hidden from the vicissitudes of daily living by learner-explorers before they become full-fledged adult practitioners.

(5) Hidden Space demonstrates that Social Space may contain riches beyond those immediately recognized. Any attempt to make an inventory of a society's actual riches – such as economic capital, social capital, and cultural capital – quickly shows that there is a huge amount of information and original thinking to be drawn upon (such as Robert Putnam's about Social Capital being crucial to a society's internal cohesion and the rich scholarship in the wake of that insight). It leaves me with the sense that it would be foolish, at this time, to even attempt to offer such an "inventory." Yet the

riches of Social Space must be acknowledged. They are real. But the precise articulation of their content and nature is still a work in progress.

(6) Hidden Space preserves potentially dangerous and destructive culture content, keeping it available for activation. Here extreme racism, extreme anti-Semitism, and religious zealotry come to mind. In recent history, all of these have in fact been activated, when "Western Modernism" had assumed that they had long ago been superseded by more progressive ways of thinking and behaving. It turns out that they had not been superseded and eliminated but, instead, had been retained in hidden storage – and were available for activation. Their activation took many forms. There was the public, nationalistic form of Nazi anti-Semitism. There was the Shiite-Sunni form of lethal conflicts in the Near East. There was the subterranean version of American anti-Obama-presidency hysteria. All of these suggest that while in a hidden condition, a culture component may grow in grotesquely anti-social form (as regarded by the prevailing culture) yet continue to grow ever-more extreme, since there was no public awareness, supervision, and control of it during its hidden state.

CLOSED SPACE:

The Moral World Phenomenon

I. Thesis

We humans exist in moral contexts. *For individuals*: Amid the rhythm of our daily life, we usually have in mind, even when we do not consciously formulate it, some sort of moral context that guides us. From it one can derive a sense of purpose and meaning for one's life. The social psychologist Jonathan Haidt examined this in his book "The Righteous Mind." *For societies*: Almost a century ago the sociologist Emile Durkheim taught us that human societies are built on shared moral systems. They create a society's cohesion. They are its building blocks. They are what makes a community a community; a society a society. Actually, Jonathan Haidt is a Durkheimian, who understands very well the conjoint nature of the individual and the societal – while his posture is to understand a society from the viewpoint of the participating individual.

Behind this benign feature there is another, far less benign feature. One moral context can vehemently exclude other moral contexts. It can be a Closed Moral Space – negating what, morally, is outside that space, while honoring what, morally, is inside that space. Here there is no weighing of alternative moralities. Indeed, alternatives are apt to be decisively excluded, as illegitimate, as unworthy of existing. This is the Closed Moral World phenomenon – a Social Space where wars against the morally other are readily justified.

II. Elaboration

An overview --

To understand the moral context issues I shall begin by turning to the famous Milgram electric shock experiments.[20] In these experiments Stanley Milgram succeeded in excluding the outside world's prevailing morality and, in its place, substituted an entirely different morality. This established a Closed Moral World, within which grossly immoral behavior, even from the participants' own point of view, could take place. Yet it was carried out by these very same participants, whose moral upbringing was being violated.

Similarly, I shall review Christopher Browning's study of German police reservists who became mass murderers (described in his book, *Ordinary Men*[21].) This, too, will be shown to have been a Closed Moral World – within which formerly unthinkable behavior became thinkable, doable, and, from the participants' point of view, morally justified.

Thirdly, I shall briefly discuss the jihadist followers of Abu Musab Zarqarwi, the cultivation of terrorism by the use of the Web and, most alarmingly, the recruiting of suicide bombers on supposedly moral grounds.

The seductive power of Closed Moral Worlds is the issue. These Moral Worlds combine the exclusion, in ongoing situations, of much of the external world's morality – even the participants' own moral upbringing – while opening up an entirely new venue for moral behavior within these situations. In that new venue participants believe they are making a moral contribution to a morally justified cause. Seduction, indeed.

Finally, I shall discuss a very different feature of Closed Moral Worlds, one in which we frequently find ourselves. Namely, that Closed Moral Worlds can enable us to live with uncertainty – with not knowing things that affect us crucially, but we can continue to function. Our social existence includes quite specific societal techniques for coping with, and taking advantage of, not knowing. All this happens under moral umbrellas within our Social Space.

More elaboration:
The Milgram experiments –
How Closed Moral Worlds seduce us

In the history of twentieth-century psychology, the Milgram experiments stand out as possibly the most imaginative and courageous of all experimental research on human behavior. To be sure there was Ivan Pavlov's even more famous work on conditioning, performed on dogs, for which he was awarded the Nobel Prize for Physiology and Medicine in 1904, as well as the work of numerous other creative and insightful researchers into psychological features of behavior. However Milgram's experiments stand out because they tough-mindedly addressed an issue that tormented the entire civilized world after the horrors of the Nazi era. That issue was the fact that the citizens of a highly "civilized" nation, modern Germany, had created and actually carried out an organized program of mass brutality that was unmatched in recorded human history. How could this happen? Was it based on something unique to Germany – its culture and upbringing in the notorious German "authoritarian personality"? Perhaps Germans were uniquely prone to obeying authority, according to the popular stereotype of the upbringing and behavior of Germans? If so, then presumably Americans would not be so obedience-prone. Milgram's experiments were designed to test this issue by examining obedience to authority among Americans.

Briefly stated, Stanley Milgram invited and paid individuals to participate in an experiment that was supposedly concerned with how people remember and learn. At the time, in the 1960s, Milgram was on the faculty of Yale University. Under the mantle of academic research and with the blessing and sponsorship of that great university, the research was promoted to prospective participants.

The actual procedure included an "experimenter," a "learner," and a "subject" (cast in the role of teacher). The exercise consisted of the subject reading a series of paired words and then reading one of the paired words and asking the learner to recall the appropriate matched paired word. The learner was hooked up to an electronic connection. In Milgram's own words, "the subject was told to administer a shock to the learner each time he gave a wrong response. Moreover – and this is the key command – the subject was instructed to 'move one level higher on the shock generator each time the learner gives a wrong answer.' He was also instructed to announce the voltage level before administering a shock. This served to incrementally remind the subject of the increasing intensity of shocks administered by the learner."[22]

In reality, there was no electrical current. No shock was actually given. The experimenter and learner were actors. It merely appeared that when the learner made mistakes, he actually received an electric shock. As the shocks escalated, due to the increasing "mistakes" by the role-playing learner, he cried out in "agony." But the subject –the "teacher" – was not an actor! That person was terribly – and terrifyingly – real. He actually believed that he was administering electric shocks to the inept learner.

The unanticipated and amazing result turned out to be that most subjects were willing to administer electric shocks to the learner. Despite expressing qualms of conscience, most of them kept on escalating the level of shock as the learner was crying out in "pain" when receiving ever-higher levels of shock, because of continuing to make mistakes. The experimenter continued to tell the subjects that they simply had to continue to follow instructions – the scientific fate of the experiment depended on them doing so.

In Milgram's experiment many different individuals participated as subjects. The experiments were repeated in many different settings, even in different countries. In each study, there were a few exceptional subjects. In Milgram's own laboratory, one of those who refused to inflict pain was a woman of German background. But the majority of individuals – ordinary people, not hand-picked sadists – went along with the instructions and were willing to inflict pain on entirely innocent people.

Clearly, Milgram rightly maintains, it turns out that obedience to authority – leading to horrendous behavior – was not simply a German phenomenon.

Quite ordinary people, almost everywhere, seem fully capable of doing such things.

In the post-World War II milieu – where people were still trying to come to grips with the Holocaust and other atrocities – this was not a happy finding. Stanley Milgram received his share of opprobrium to the extent that he sometimes expressed regret that he ever undertook this work. Yet scientifically and objectively there seems little doubt that his findings stand up and must be taken seriously.

In recent years there have been many other indications that "ordinary people" are quite willing to take part in horrendous activities. All these findings are indebted to Milgram's work. His findings are being borne out again and again (in a moment I shall take up a prominent example, the study by the historian Christopher Browning). Yet the mind still boggles at the idea of ordinary people – who are not sick or demented – doing horrendous things to others. Factually we know that this happens. Intellectually we are still bewildered. For this reason it is necessary to dig more deeply into Milgram's experiments and go beyond what Milgram himself thought his experiments were all about.

I shall claim that the crucial feature of the experiments was that, in the confines of the laboratory where the experiments took place, Milgram succeeded in replacing the outside world's morality – on which the participants were brought up – and, in its place, substituted an entirely different morality. He thereby created a Closed Moral Space, with a morality of its own.

Through his various psychological manipulations Stanley Milgram created a Closed Moral Space in the laboratory. It created a specific moral context for the participating individuals, the "subjects." Their external moral worlds – their home lives, personal upbringing and values, and their various other affiliations and allegiances – were declared out of bounds, irrelevant and inappropriate. Participants were told that here, in the laboratory, a system of morality existed that fully governed what went on. It was a distinctive and complete moral system that must be adhered to in order to achieve the very noble ends of the scientific experiment. This moral space was limited to the moral order in which they found themselves while they were in the laboratory. Moral myopia prevailed. Morally speaking, it was a Closed World.

Individual participants occasionally tried to bring in their outside values. They complained that it was dangerous and bad to be hurting the "learner." Each time this happened, such concerns were decisively and totally overruled by the experimenter.

The striking thing is how successful Milgram was in creating such a Closed Moral Space. There is no indication that he intended to create one. But, nonetheless, he seems to have succeeded in doing so.

The upshot of what one must deduce from Milgram's results is that the grotesquely inhuman actions of the Nazi German era, the genocide of millions of innocent persons, are not a uniquely "German authoritarian personality" phenomenon. It turns out that, to understand the genocide, we have to look at the Social Space that permeated Germany before and during the Hitler regime. Germany's "modernism" had not eliminated anti-Semitism but merely stored it – as I suggested in the previous chapter. In addition, however, there occurred the exuberant emergence of a Closed Moral World – where, amid zealous nationalism, murderous anti-Semitism received "moral" blessing. Within that fantasized moral world, Jews are claimed to be the single greatest obstacle to Germany's pure Aryan destiny, as well as Germany achieving her rightful national pre-eminence – which, thanks to Hitler's leadership, would finally be within reach. Germany was in a moral crusade. That crusade brooked no questioning. It received widespread support in the German nation.

Here, then, is a very different explanation of Milgram's own view of his findings – that the issue is, first and foremost, the obedience-to-authority syndrome. The difference between Milgram's explanation and mine is nowhere more explicit than in the application to the notorious My Lai massacre during the Vietnam War. There, it is clear, a nascent and distinctive moral space came into existence. It happened as follows:

One day at My Lai, a small village in Vietnam, several hundred unarmed civilians were killed by American soldiers. When this became known it aroused widespread reaction, including efforts by scholars to try to understand how this could have happened. Milgram's explanation of the My Lai massacre was to focus on obedience to authority. He emphasized that the participating soldiers, in their obedience to authority, utterly abandoned their moral responsibilities, becoming virtual automatons who acted thoughtlessly.[23]

By contrast, I suggest that the soldiers at My Lai created a new moral space. In it flourished a very distinctive culture, a culture of exuberant killing. It began immediately after the troops landed at My Lai. It lasted about five hours. The culture operated as a Closed Moral World, totally oblivious to the civilian world and any of its rules of humane conduct. It had internal dynamics and structure. It had a "morality" of its own. Within it, the participating soldiers acted with distinct objectives: every living thing, including animals, was fair game for killing. Rewards were at hand: Some soldiers bragged about their innovative killing techniques, knowing they would get a favorable response from their fellow solders.

In that nascent moral space, shared motivations were at work, fostering the culture of exuberant killing. They became the fuel that generated it and the energy that sustained it during its five-hour existence. What were these motivations? Previously the enemy had frequently ambushed American soldiers, with murderous results – and had done so with impunity because that enemy could not be found and pinned down for a fight. Finally, finally, one was doing something about the elusive enemy who, after ambushing American soldiers, had committed atrocities against them. These atrocities, almost too painful to describe, included exhibiting the mutilated bodies of American soldiers, one's buddies, and placing them so that they would later be found by their American comrades, after these comrades had listened to the nightly screams as their buddies were being tortured. This produced radical reactions. The participating American soldiers at My Lai were venting their pent-up rage. They felt amply justified in what they were now doing. They were creating a new moral space for their actions.

The American soldiers at My Lai, far from being automatons, as Milgram believed, acted with focused energy, with zeal and joy, with creativity – within a nascent Closed Moral Space. They felt they were doing the right thing (as Milgram himself cited). They were operating in the confines of distinctive, locally generated rules of conduct, a morality of its own. The content of that morality – with its focus on exuberant killing – may strike us as appalling. But in its own perverse way there was indeed a system of morality, if by morality we mean a set of principles that guide human behavior. It was "closed" in that any other morality was irrelevant. For these soldiers, their current moral space was the only one that counted.

Let us return to the Milgram experiments and their guiding paradigm. It not only has particular options and distinctive blinders as to what is and what is not legitimate science. It also has links to an outside reality, a larger vision of what is relevant and important to the paradigm.

In Milgram's paradigm the larger outside reality included horrors perpetrated by Germany under the Nazi regime. Here was an extremely authoritarian government and a country where authority was worshipped. Surely obedience to authority must be more fully understood. Perhaps it will present us with as clue as to how such suffering could be created in our own time and perhaps prevented in the future. In the personal case of Stanley Milgram, that suffering had victimized his fellow Jews most of all. Deception seemed a justified option in his search, even if it involved blinders to some venerable moral issues, including both lying to the subjects and persuading them to engage in immoral acts. After all, this research was addressing fundamental aspects of human behavior. From the knowledge gained, perhaps another Holocaust could be prevented.

In the paradigm Milgram bestowed onto the subjects of his experiment, the link to a larger vision consisted of sharing, for one fleeting moment, in the prestige of a prominent university and the world of science. It produced the justification for doing things one would ordinarily not do. It supplied blinders by disallowing one's personal moral standards while one was within the 'community of science.'

In the Closed Moral World paradigm I am proposing to explain the Milgram findings there is also a link to a larger vision. Namely that humans – as individuals and as members of a society – are moral creatures. As individuals: We get our sense of who we are, what our life is all about, from perceiving that we are linked to a moral context that gives meaning to our life. This can include a formulation such as "I am an American, I vote and pay my taxes," where "being an American" is a statement that identifies a particular version of morality, to which the individual is making a morally justified contribution. As members of a society: The core of the human society in which we live is brought to us by the social institutions that identify its moral consensus. Much depends on how that moral consensus is spelled out, implemented, and brought to us by the social institutions of the society in which we live. (The moral consensus can include such social institutions as monogamous marriage and democratically elected heads of the government.)

The individual is heavily involved in implementing Closed Moral Worlds.

We attain a sense of personal moral virility from actually making a contribution to a moral world. Within that world we see our options. From this comes the seductiveness of a moral world. We envision the rewards derived from our own contribution. We are, after all, about to enrich the moral world to which we subscribe and contribute.

The Milgram subjects were made to feel that they were making a moral contribution to a moral world. They were embraced by a deliberately created morality. Through it they became personally linked, in their own minds, to the pursuit of larger moral goals. Through their own contribution to that pursuit, participants were exercising moral virility. To be sure they bought this at a price – namely the application of blinders to their personal moral upbringing. Instead, they were exercising their option to contribute to something they had come to regard as noble and important.

Milgram reports that the subjects occasionally felt and expressed great discomfort about inflicting electric shocks on the "learner." Yet they continued to inflict them. Here is an example: A subject tells the experimenter, "He [the learner] can't stand it. I am not going to kill that man in there. You hear him hollering in there? He's hollering. He can't stand it."[24] The subject desperately wants to stop administering shocks, but he continues to do so. Clearly there is a binding constraint on him not based on physical force. No one is physically forcing him to continue. It is a moral force, a binding moral bond. In the laboratory a moral community has come into existence. In that community any deviation is seen as a moral transgression.[25] One would be breaking with one's moral obligation if one stopped administering the electric shocks to the screaming learner.

In this local moral community distinctive obligations prevail. These are reinforced by the explicit directives from the experimenter. He tells the subject that he simply must continue to administer shocks, regardless of the anguish and pain of the learner. Moral obligations are also buttressed by situational etiquette (this is Milgram's term, based on the work of Erving Goffman) where, within the confines of an ongoing situation, it becomes increasingly difficult to change one's behavior. The subject has promised to follow instructions.

One cannot lightly break one's promise. One is bound, socially and morally, to an obligation to the experimenter personally, as well as to the entire program. Such values as loyalty, dependability, and honesty are invoked to keep one in line. One is, in short, a member of a moral community – based on moral bonding among its members – where in return for moral rewards there are also distinctive moral obligations. In the moral community that prevails in this social space, moral bindings accompany moral bonding.

The above example of Milgram's subjects expressing discomfort about inflicting pain on innocent persons should not deflect us from realizing that the majority of these subjects completed their participation in the experiments. They expressed satisfaction that they had contributed to important work. They were satisfied with their participation. They felt that their activity in the experiment was entirely worthwhile. Although they did not use these terms, they indicate that what they did was morally justified.

In a larger sense Milgram created a Closed World within the Social Space of life in the laboratory. Its sinews were moral bonds among its members.

That Closed World asserts itself by shutting out the moral authority of anything outside of its own boundaries. It becomes blind to competing moralities. But in exchange it offers the participants a chance to celebrate their moral virility, provided they do so within the confines of the Closed Moral World.

One must not assume that in the Closed Moral World, as exemplified in the Milgram experiments, the values of the outside world are magically and totally excluded. More accurately, when allowed to enter, they are likely to be subverted through repackaging. As already mentioned, many subjects in the experiment retained great misgivings about shocking innocent persons. Their outside values were still real to them. Yet they told themselves "they could not muster the inner resources to translate their values into action."[26]

The subjects felt bound by the system. Still, given their misgivings, some "derived satisfaction from their [negative] thoughts and felt that – within themselves, at least – they had been on the side of the angels."[27] In short, they were using their own discretion to manufacture a rationalization for participating in the system. They did so by acknowledging their outside values, though in a most convoluted form. In a way, they were thereby making the horror system work, by repackaging their outside values in such a way that they could live with themselves while engaging in behavior that was diametrically opposed to their values. Thereby the participants turned these values into instruments for supporting the system of horror.

I first encountered this way of rationalizing gruesome behavior while studying Rudolf Hoess, the man in charge of the Auschwitz concentration camp. He, too, claimed to be appalled by the brutalities going on at Auschwitz!!! I tend to believe him – that, in his own mind, he was appalled. But I am also convinced that his ways of rationalizing were a major instrument for producing the brutalities. He, more than anyone else, was responsible for fostering them, while convincing himself that he remained a humane human being.

In the Milgram program of research, the experimenter was willing to invoke outside values – such as loyalty, dependability and honesty – to ensure the continuation of the horrors. In short, outside values were allowed to intrude into the Closed Moral World of the Milgram experiments. But they did so in a highly selective way. They were repackaged through the machinations of the experimenter and the inadvertent collusion of the subjects. In this way the Closed Moral World imprinted its distinctive character on the behavior of the participants.

Next, let us examine Christopher Browning's report on even more harrowing human behavior. He does so in his book "Ordinary Men." What he found is in keeping with Milgram's findings – that ordinary people can be induced to do horrendous deeds. But in contrast to Milgram's report of behavior in an artificially contrived Social Space, in a laboratory, Browning reports on actual, deliberate, mass-murdering behavior. It was carried out by German soldiers, acting publicly, under military directives, during their tour of duty in Poland. It happened in an actual (not artificially created) Social Space. Before I go into specifics, here are a few words about the broader picture. The behavior of these German soldiers took the form of deliberate, systematic murder of innocent persons. They did so while they were operating under official military directives. They did so, also, within the prevailing ideology of Nazism, where the elimination of supposed enemies – even their mass murder – was officially sanctioned. These combined to form their "moral" underpinning, in the form of a specific, prevailing Closed Moral World. It produced the mandate to implement the mass murders. It nurtured their murderous deeds. In short there, in Poland, the soldiers were operating in a Social Space where a Closed Moral World underwrote their campaign of mass murders.

Now the specifics: In his book Browning describes the actions of a battalion of German police reservists, based in Hamburg, who had hoped to sit out the war without having to engage in combat. They were somewhat older than the average soldier. They had respected places in their community, stable occupations, and families. They were not young fanatics. Few were Nazi party members.

Eventually the battalion of approximately five hundred men was activated for military duty and sent to Poland. On arrival there the battalion was assigned the task of carrying out mass extermination of Jews – killing these innocent people who inhabited villages in the region around the town of Lublin. Initially individual members of the battalion were given the option not to participate. But virtually all of them did participate. They did not choose the option of not participating. The majority – Browning estimates between eighty and ninety percent – went ahead and carried out the killings. Some did it with reluctance. Some did it with zeal. Most of them merely complied with the prevailing ways.

With these findings Browning guides into a terrifying world: Ordinary people – whom we cannot write off as sadists, poisoned anti-Semites, or ethnic zealots -- could, and did, engage in mass killings of innocent people.

But Browning provides no good answer to how-could-this-have-happened? What was going on? My objective is to answer these questions, going beyond the Milgram theme (and Browning's opinion) of obedience-to-authority being at the core of it all -- that the soldiers were merely obeying orders.

Although I have been wrestling with this same issue for some years, and have published a book about it,[28] I have great difficulty citing and addressing Browning's revelations. The area of Poland to which the reservists were sent in June 1942, and where they carried out their murderous activities, is the vicinity where my own father and mother and all remaining Jews from my German village were sent in April 1942. They died there, at Izbica. My older brother, having immigrated to Holland, but captured there by the invading Germans, was also sent to that region. He died at the Sobibor concentration camp. Even though Browning does not specifically mention my loved ones, he describes their fate. With their memory in mind and my obligation to them, I undertake the distasteful task of building on Browning's work. And importantly, that we are still disconcertingly short of really convincing and adequate explanations of how such horrors could, and did happen.

I come to Browning's depictions from the conviction that even such horrors as he describes are not beyond our capacity to understand. We need to create, and *we can_create*, the appropriate conceptual tools, the ways of looking so that we may see more clearly. By seeing more clearly, we may eventually create effective weapons against such horrors.

First and foremost, the members of the Reserve Battalion 101 were molded into a cohesive community, containing an increasingly Closed Moral World. This was achieved through their common training and association with one another before they left Hamburg; and by their relatively constant membership in their battalion; and above all, by being removed together from their home setting and relocated to the Lublin area of Poland. There they formed an enclave of their own. They were now physically separated from their home and culturally released from many of their home constraints. It was their first field assignment. Here a new moral community could, and did flourish. It developed its own customs and system of where each man fits. Here the duties and obligations of soldiers to one another can override more abstract notions of morality, as it does for many military units actively engaged in combat against an enemy. Immediacy prevails in the form of new, locally generated standards of morality, loyalty, and decency.

For example, Browning reports that it became a soldier's obligation to become "a shooter" – a killer in a very explicit way. Those who were still appalled by this role and tried to evade it tended to explain their reluctance to shoot as their own "weakness" rather than the moral degeneracy of that "obligation." In short, even these "deviants" were upholding the local morality, in which it was one's obligation – one's moral obligation – to shoot designated people. Often the reluctant shooters were told by their comrades that shooting was everyone's obligation. By not shooting they were doing damage to the whole unit. They were evading their personal obligation to the group and its mission.

Carrying out this obligation underscored one's good standing in this community – as a good soldier who can be counted on to do his share of the task. It also added to one's stature. Precisely because the mission was onerous, one's shootings were making a noble contribution, demonstrating one's moral virility. It was but a short step to demonstrating zeal in the fine art of killing. Even those who began with moral scruples against personally carrying out killings could become proficient and no longer reluctant shooters-to-kill. They were drawn into a system with its own set of rewards. Being regarded as a good soldier is about as high an honor as you can hope to achieve in the confines of this Closed Moral World. Killings could be carried our without anesthetizing liquor. One could come to enjoy killing. Even those who did not become zealots tended to accept the obligation – to kill designated people – on the moral ground that prevailed in the Social Space in which the soldiers operated.

There was room for different forms of participation. Browning reports that there "emerged within Reserve Battalion 101: a nucleus of increasingly enthusiastic killers who volunteered for the firing squads and "Jew hunts"; a larger group … who performed as shooters and ghetto clearers when assigned but did not seek opportunities to kill (and in some cases refrained from killing, contrary to standing orders, when no one was monitoring their actions); and a small group (less than twenty percent) of refusers and evaders."[28] Even the latter tended to classify themselves as weaklings, thereby honoring the prevailing morality in their military unit.

At the heart of the tragedy is that the majority of participants came to regard their actions as morally justified, at least at the time of their participation. The rest of us, living in a very different moral milieu, find this appalling. But our reaction must not blind us. The reality is that we are all morally nurtured creatures, living in a Social Space where, at any time, a particular morality is apt to prevail. We require a moral context for our own sense of who and what we are. And most importantly, through our own active contribution to that moral context, we create our sense of moral virility, our sense of being alive and worthy of being alive. All this is normal and "ordinary."

What distinguishes the police battalion's actions is that they are a moral mutation from their own moral background. It was fostered in a particular Social Space, namely the battalion's Polish setting and everything that came with it. These produced a particular morality, quite different from the morality of their upbringing at home. It was dominated by the imprint of the local context. Despite this difference from their past, the new local morality prevailed.

Moral mutations such as these are not unusual. They arise from the particular circumstances at hand. In the case of the police reservist battalion, they are the fact of being sent to Poland, and there given the murderous mission of annihilating entire sections of the local Jewish population. They then carry out that assignment – and build the moral tools with which to do it. These tools mold the reservists into a community of individuals with shared commitment and focus. This process harnesses normal human attributes, notably those of gearing one's own moral virility to the task at hand. This created a new moral configuration, one that is permeated by a locally generated, constricted vision of the world, where a morality can come to prevail that is utterly at variance with the outside world from which the participants come. It is a Closed Moral World, nurtured by a Social Space.

If one were to restrict oneself to the Milgram orientation, one might be inclined to say that, as good Germans, these police reservists were simply obeying orders. Yet I would say that a more persuasive view is that these men, just as the subjects in the Milgram experiments, developed and operated within a Closed Moral World, which produced a distinctive moral vision for them. And which, in turn, was fostered by the particular Social Space within which the participants operated.

The lesson one must learn is that Social Spaces can be created where "good" individuals – who are not morally depraved to begin with, who are not sick in any clinical sense, who are not deviants or misfits – will do horrendous deeds. The participants are not being brainwashed, coerced, or seduced into unquestioning obedience. On the contrary, Social Spaces can be created so that individuals will gladly, willingly, and "morally" engage in horrors. The seduction derives from the fact that Social Spaces can offer themselves as venues for effective living, for personal fulfillment, for reaching out to life itself amid a social community.

In the year 2005 the West received a jolting wake-up call from the jihadist followers of Abu Musab Zarqawi. In Iraq these followers were carrying out suicide attacks on an unprecedented scale. They were waging war against the West by using their own bodies, combined with highly sophisticated use of the Internet. The latter is developing into an entirely new method of warfare.[29]

That new method includes the deliberate flaunting of values that are counter those of the West. A glaring example was not merely the beheading of Western victims, but videotaping the beheadings and distributing them in worldwide forums through the Internet – promoting the viewpoint that these were not merely acts of killing but supposedly justified acts of slaughtering animals.

The new method of warfare includes bonding that does not require face-to-face interaction. It can, nonetheless, create strong ties that can, literally, traverse the entire globe. The ties are accomplished by using broadband and other recent developments in technology that enable very rapid and sophisticated communication. The content of all this communicating includes veneration of suicide bombers by posting their detailed biographies; posting recipes for suicide bomb actions; and documenting suicide bombings while they happen. It is all happening in Social Space, located largely in Cyberspace.

The new method of warfare includes recruiting suicide bombers not only from the dispossessed, but also from well-educated, middle-class persons, from individuals with a spouse and children and holding good jobs. (Here I am reminded of Hitler being able to get well-to-do and educated Germans to cooperate in his murderous programs.) How is this possible?

Behind such recruitment, is there a core message?

I believe we are seeing the workings of a particular kind of Social Space, where Closed Moral Worlds are embraced. In it a Hitler, a Zarqawi, or a leader of a cult is accepted as a harbinger of access to Ultimates. Zarqawi, just as Hitler or a cult leader, identifies the Ultimate, the very greatest good and the very greatest evil, and declares that this Ultimate is within your reach. You, personally, can make a profound impact on it. Practically, Zarqawi identifies the Great Satan –America, and everything it stands for – as the Ultimate evil, and you, through your act of suicide bombing, are grabbing that Satan by the throat and throttling him. You, personally, are making it happen. Your matrimony with the Ultimate is something for which leaving your wife and small children is a small price to pay.

Hitler did the same. During his rise to power he gave spell-binding speeches that supposedly identified the Ultimate evils – Jews and international enemies that had unfairly punished Germany after the First World War – and invited Germans to join the crusade against such Ultimate evil and thereby return Germans to national glory and grandeur. You, the citizen of Germany, can join that crusade and make it happen. And many Germans did join; and they did try to make it happen. It all took place in a Social Space that embraced Closed Moral Worlds, such as the one we saw among the police reservists.

III. Assessment

(i.) Destructive Closed Moral Worlds do happen

The Thesis stated, in a rather theoretical, abstract way, that within a Social Space a Closed Moral World can provide an individual's basis of belonging to something greater than oneself – as well as producing the basic building blocks of a society, of what holds it together. But also, that such Closed Moral Worlds can harbor a sense of exclusiveness, where other moralities are decisively excluded.

The Elaboration focused on the latter of these issues. It did so by re-assessing research findings by the scholars Stanley Milgram and Christopher Browning.

The findings by these researchers leads one to realize that a Social Space can nurture a Closed Moral World that is astoundingly divorced from reverence for life and a sense of decency that had presumably been achieved – and prevailed – in modern societies. The wider issue is how are massive assaults on human dignity, decency, and reverence of life societally sponsored? How is it that such behavior cannot only happen, but is underwritten by a society's moral building blocks? We found that it not only CAN HAPPEN but that it DOES HAPPEN, given Closed Moral Worlds that can be fostered and enshrined in a Social Space – perhaps temporarily, perhaps long-term.

I shall assume – but not develop here – that at other times, in other circumstances, we could discover other Closed Moral Worlds underwriting other forms of ghastly behavior. Let me just mention, however, that in our time we have the followers of ISIS finding "moral justification" – in the shape of a Closed Moral World within deliberately created Social Space – of beheading non-adherents to their particular faith.

The issue, in all of these, is that Social Space – in which we humans organize our social existence – can nurture widely varying forms of Closed Moral Worlds. The preceding pages showed such nurture can really happen – in an artificially contrived laboratory and in the actual, open world.

III. Assessment

(ii) Closed Moral Worlds are vulnerable

Amid the apparent power and success of a Closed Moral World such as Zarquawi's, one must ask: Will it continue its pernicious course forever? How will it end? I do not know the answer to these questions. But I do believe there are inherent vulnerabilities within Closed Moral Worlds that my lead to their demise. Internally, within Closed Moral Worlds, there can be a process of ever-increasing escalation of its uniqueness, of its difference from the surrounding world – such as flaunting the beheading of Westerners – that will lead to increasing estrangement from the rest of the world. These escalations are seemingly unstoppable, sometimes growing to grotesque levels because the Closed Moral World is totally turned inwards, looking for ever-greater ways to assert its existence as a separate and unique entity.

I am reminded (1) of the French Revolution, where the revolutionaries began by sending external enemies to the guillotine and then, in a process of internal escalation of moral rectitude, began sending its own members to the guillotine. And (2) of Hitler's ever-increasing risk-taking ventures, notably his decision to invade the Soviet Union. He was already at war with the largest Western nations, winter was approaching, the German army was not equipped with winter clothing, in the past the vast snow-laden territory of the Soviet Union had become a graveyard for many a previous foreign invader. Still, Hitler went ahead and ordered the war against the Soviet Union.

I realize that internal escalation of content in an existing Closed Moral World is not a precise prediction of what will happen. I am merely pointing to a vulnerability in the very nature of Closed Moral Worlds: That by escalating their uniqueness they contribute to their increasing estrangement for their surrounding world, and eventually alienated responses from that world are apt to accumulate.

Let us also remind ourselves that a seemingly invincible Closed Moral World is on occasion punctured by a single event. I recall that at height of Senator Joseph McCarthy's reign of terror on the American scene, where an apparently Closed Moral World, with its very own set of rules and objectives, was often on display during Senate hearings. The Senator often attacked vulnerable, innocent individuals, and did so with seeming impunity. However, during one such hearing an elderly, dignified defense lawyer, Mr. Joseph Welch, said: "Have you no sense of decency, Sir? At long last, have you left no sense of decency?" At that moment the McCarthy movement came to an end. Many cowed politicians now found the courage to speak up against the Senator. Senator McCarthy was eventually censured by the Senate, citing many excesses in his use of power. McCarthy's balloon was suddenly punctured, never to fly again.

Why the particular statement by Mr. Welch had such transforming impact, why it was a tipping point, is not known. But its impact was beyond doubt. A colossal juggernaut of destructive behavior – within a seeming Morality of its own – was suddenly halted. It seems that Closed Moral Worlds do contain vulnerabilities. Inherent in their internally escalating their uniqueness they may, eventually, foster an external reaction.

III. Assessment

(iii) A particular kind of Closed Moral World: It underwrites needed zones of not-knowing.

For example: The doctor-patient relationship

I go to my doctor and talk about my various symptoms – let's say the aches and pains in my stomach, my lost appetite, the changes in my bodily functioning, my difficulty sleeping, and so forth. The doctor will listen to me, ask me further questions, examine me physically (and, a bit, mentally: am I to be taken seriously or am I just another nut-case who comes with different "symptoms" every week?). The doctor will check my vital signs and possibly arrange for some laboratory tests. I know the general routine, even though I am not a medical doctor.

I do not know what diagnosis for my symptoms the doctor will actually produce. After all producing a diagnosis – and a strategy for doing something about it – is the doctor's job, not mine. If I already knew the diagnosis and a corrective course of action, I would not need to go to the doctor.

I also do not know, beforehand, what the doctor's demeanor will be during my visit. Is the doctor hurried or slow, harried or relaxed, pleasant or abrupt? Does the doctor's sudden furrowed brow indicate alarm about my condition or recall a recent poor performance on a golf course? The list of my efforts to interpret the doctor's demeanor could go on.

The doctor's demeanor can play a crucial psychological-projective role. Many patients describe their own condition in terms of the doctor's supposed feelings: "The doctor was happy with the results of the tests"; "The doctor was concerned, so there need to be more tests."

I do not know what the doctor will actually say to me. (That is why it is important to bring along someone – a spouse, a significant other, a friend –since in your agitated state you are not likely to remember what the doctor actually said. Given your state of anxiety, you are likely to hear, and recall, the doctor's words very selectively and inaccurately. The person I have brought along is part of my knowledge management process.)

In short, there is a lot of uncertainty in the interaction between the doctor and me. There is much about the doctor's response to me that I do not know beforehand. The doctor's demeanor, as we talk, is largely an enigma. More important, I cannot predict the doctor's exact response to me and my symptoms. I do not know what fate of mine is being unearthed in the doctor's office, or how the doctor will unearth it, or how it will be presented to me.

Yet all is not lost or sour. There is a great deal about the doctor I do know. I know that medical criteria are supposed to prevail as the doctor makes a judgment about me and my symptoms: not whether I am a nice person, whether or not the doctor likes me, whether or not the doctor is influenced by my economic circumstances, whether the doctor approves of my moral behavior, whether the doctor resents people of my religion or ethnicity. None of these are supposed to enter the doctor's judgment of what is going on in my stomach (with the exception that my ethnic-based eating habits may reveal a clue about my stomach troubles). Medical criteria include – if the doctor is in the mainstream of Western medicine – the generally accepted content of Western scientific medicine and how these are implemented in the physician's professional life. In fact, being a medical professional means that the physician is a guardian of a body of scientific medical knowledge. There are strict rules of how that knowledge is to be deployed. These rules include the very items I just mentioned on the negative side: what doctors should not consider while making a medical judgment. On the positive side, the rules govern use and implementation of a body of scientific knowledge. The doctor is expected not only to know the basics from medical training but keep up with developments. I, as the patient, do not know the specifics about medical science that govern the professional activities of the doctor. But I do know the general principle that medical criteria are supposed to prevail in my doctor's behavior toward me. And I know that there are enforcement mechanisms should the doctor depart from these criteria. If, for example, the doctor were to discriminate against me because I am of an ethnic group the doctor does not like, then I would have recourse against that doctor.

There is a larger process behind the transaction I have just described. The doctor's unpredictable behavior means that there is discretion by that doctor as to what is said to the patient and, more importantly, how to proceed to come up with a diagnosis and treatment strategy for that patient. This discretion – I sometimes call it a zone of autonomy – means that the doctor can mobilize any information deemed relevant to the particular circumstances of the particular patient now sitting in the doctor's office. This autonomy, this discretion, is absolutely crucial if the doctor is to have the flexibility to devise, in his professional judgment, the most appropriate diagnosis and strategy for treating the patient's impaired health. There is a trade-off. The doctor has a zone of discretion to mobilize the available medical knowledge. In exchange, the patient grants the doctor a zone of action, of autonomy, in a particular sector where I, the patient, do not know what will be produced. But I get the benefit of the mobilization of medical knowledge on my behalf.

The upshot of this example is that in my relationship to the doctor there is quite a lot of unpredictable behavior. But I, as patient, can accept this because I know the limits within which the unpredictable behavior can exist. I know these limits quite clearly: medical criteria, and nothing else, should guide conduct. These criteria are known to me informally. And they are spelled out legally in the formal rules that govern the practice of medicine in this and most countries where Western medicine is permitted to be practiced.

My use of the doctor-patient analogy is a technique for drawing attention to a feature behind much of human social behavior. Not-knowing is not necessarily a bad thing. It may in fact be crucially important and necessary. Stated a bit more formally: Unpredictable behavior can be a necessary part of a social transaction when it operates within known limits. Knowing the limits enables the participants to continue to interact with one another. This applies to many different circumstances.

Virtually every professional is involved in unpredictable behavior that is socially protected when operating within known limits. The schoolteacher, social worker, architect, and engineer are all licensed to operate within legally defined rules. Within such rules, they enjoy considerable necessary freedom of action. Within stated limits, they can make decisions that adapt and apply their specialized knowledge to tackling issues they encounter in the course of their professional work. And these zones of unpredictability for professionals carry with it zones of the unknown for the clients of these professionals. Both are necessary!

Also, there are highly unpredictable career paths, such as the scientist pursuing research into the currently unknown, using science whose limits, in the form of the reigning paradigm, are known. That paradigm spells out what are regarded as legitimate topics to investigate, legitimate techniques for doing research, and legitimate ways of communicating one's findings. Paradigms are limit statements – within which creative activity is possible.

The following is an example of a paradigm in action in the hands of a creative scientist, and the roundabout way I came to hear about it. Above my desk I have a sign that reads 606. It reminds me of Nobel Prize winner Paul Ehrlich's discovery of the first effective drug against syphilis, in the early part of the twentieth century. He called the drug Salvarsan 606. The 606 stands for the fact that in the course of his laboratory experiments, Ehrlich experienced 605 failures before he found the one that worked. Surely Ehrlich was confronting unpredictable results as he conducted one experiment after another. But surely, too, he believed that he was onto something – that he was within the limits of legitimate science while pursuing his quest. (A personal note: During my childhood as a refugee in England I got to know Ehrlich's widow. That is how I became interested in Ehrlich as a role model, whose 606 became a motto above my desk – encouraging me not to give up in the face of many rejections.)

While writing these words I heard about the death of Jack S. Kilby, the co-inventor of the microchip. Kilby's invention created one of the most profound changes in America's and the world's national life. At the time of his invention, in the 1950s, Kilby was entirely focused on developing ways to make electrical instruments smaller. Within these limits he produced something far greater than what he himself recognized at the time. Through the limits within which he operated, focusing on making electrical instruments smaller, he created a technological revolution. Unpredictability is in full view here, but the limits – the focus on making electrical instruments smaller – made it all possible.

Of course it helped that Kilby was very persistent and very imaginative. Perhaps his failure to gain admission to MIT as a student made him try a little harder in his chosen work? Had he something to prove? Einstein's early struggle to get a respectable academic position come to mind. He, too, had to try a little harder? Each encountered limits and, perhaps perversely, drew energy from that encounter. Each eventually unleashed immense creative energy within his chosen work. And each, by his creative work, changed the paradigms – the very limits their science peers believed in – that henceforth governed physics and engineering. Perhaps, I repeat, their early encounters with limits – by Kilby not getting accepted at MIT, by Einstein not getting a university position upon graduation – encouraged them to challenge existing limits in their respective sciences.

I have drawn attention to limits-of-knowing – ranging from the empowering benefits of not-knowing to knowing its limits. This is very much part of the everyday enactment of many professions. It can also find a place in the pursuit of a career, such as a career in research science. There the unknown is directly targeted as a potentially rich source of enlightenment. The scientist does so while, typically, operating within the limits formulated in an existing paradigm. Although sometimes this may lead to changing the very limits claimed in an existing paradigm.

All these can exist in a Closed Social Space within which moral systems provide the underpinnings for professionals to practice their profession and science researchers to pursue their craft by excluding alternatives.

Transcended Space:

The Access-to-the-Ultimate phenomenon

I. Thesis

To the individual, it may seem that having access to the Ultimate is the greatest gift one can possibly receive. But societally, we need to recognize that access to the Ultimate can be nurtured in, and through the action of Social Space. There, boundaries do not exist. Instead, distant matters are accessible and active, here and now. Transcendence is at hand.

It turns out that Social Space can nurture magnificently, benign behavior. But Social Space can also nurture lethal, malignant behavior. All based on Transcendence.

II. Elaboration

Overview

I shall begin with two cases of benign transcendence: A dying woman overcoming the horrors of Auschwitz and the capacity of prayer to give us social space for highly personal transcendence. In both cases personal pain is transcended by immersion in a particular kind of Social Space.

I shall then present cases of malignant transcendence. (1) Cult members, under influence of a guru, joyfully committed suicide trying to overcome the shortcomings of their prevailing lifestyle. They did so believing that they entered a transcended space that promised them access to the Ultimate.

(2) Uglier, because it happened on such a large scale, was Hitler's Germany. Hitler promised the German people that they would overcome all the injustices heaped on them after the First World War. He, like the guru of the cult, promised Germans fulfillment of their Ultimate aspirations, transcending everything that stood in the way. (3) Finally, and sometimes ugly, are various versions of religious orthodoxy. Each version's adherents can be convinced that they – in their transcended space – are the unique and only guardians of Ultimate orthodoxy. Outside that space stand heresy, and persons unworthy of life. True believers must confront, if not smite the non-believers. Among early Christians were fervently adhered-to rival interpretations of the Jesus-based religion. Some 1500 years later saw the Thirty Years War between Protestants and Catholics. It spawned widespread destruction in the heart of Europe. It took place from 1618 to 1648, but thereafter reverberated for centuries. The most recent highlight of the zealotry phenomenon are the ISIS and Shia-Sunni conflagrations emanating form the Middle East. These indulge in exorbitant orgies of killing and mayhem that now bring us shivers.

In all the malignant transcending, Ultimate forms of cruelty found a sponsor and safe haven. It happened in a deliberately created Social Space, in the case of cults and in Hitler's Germany. And it happened in a nascent, seemingly unplanned Social Space, in the case of religious wars and zealotry.

What individual participants in malignant transcending may not recognize is that receipt of their greatest gift can come at a Faustian price, the surrender of one's soul – of all forms of decency one might once have embraced. They are now operating in a Social Space that can promote limitless zealotry – while shunning all moderation.

Benign Transcended Space: An inmate transcends the horror of the Auschwitz Concentration Camp

This is primarily the story of a dying woman at the Auschwitz concentration camp, as reported by Viktor Frankl, a psychiatrist who was himself an

55

inmate of the camp. It illustrates personal transcendence of extreme horror in one's immediate circumstances. On the verge of death, the woman discovered what is perhaps life's greatest prize, the capacity to recognize and somehow capture ultimate meaning in one's life. Her beatitude is achieved by finding a way to transcend the immediacy of her current suffering. She ends up grateful for her Auschwitz fate.

All this is described in Viktor Frankl's book, *Man's Search for Meaning: An Introduction to Logotherapy.* It is surely one of the most remarkable books to emerge from the Holocaust.[30] It is the work of a professional psychiatrist who personally experienced the horrors of Auschwitz. Here is an individual who managed to survive these horrors while maintaining moral courage and intellectual vision. After surviving Auschwitz he committed himself to sharing what he had discovered. He did so not only by caring for his patients, but by building on his experiences through research, teaching, and publication. That work is open-ended. It is always unfinished, in its wondrous examination of Transcendence (although he does not call it Transcendence. He calls it the search for Meaning). I want to honor Frankl by building within that open-ended, unfinished work about Transcendence to which he pointed us.

In his book Viktor Frankl shares the story of a young woman, an Auschwitz inmate, who knew she was going to die very soon, but who discovered in her suffering a sublime meaning in her life. Frankl, in his role as physician (and psychiatrist), approaches the dying woman and asks how she is feeling. She is lying on a bunk, facing a window through which part of a tree is visible. She is no longer able to move. She tells Frankl that she feels very well, that she is actually happier than she has ever been! She tells him that she has found great spiritual contentment in her suffering at Auschwitz – far more than she had ever experienced in her previous, rather affluent life. "I am grateful that fate has hit me so hard." And she valued the contribution of her "only friend…in my loneliness." That friend was the tree, visible through the window. She reports that she talks to the tree. Frankl, thinking she might be delirious, asks whether the tree answers her. "Oh, yes," she tells him. "It says to me, I am here – I am here – I am life, eternal life."[31]

Here, surely, is evidence of a link to a larger spiritual world that transcends the physical world – the world of pain and suffering – in which the young woman exists before her death. That spiritual world, once she accepts it, nurtures her during her existence in a world of utter desolation. It introduces a vital partnership into her desolation: She is no longer alone. In a world of endings and death, the spiritual element provides the continuity of "eternal life." The tree – within her physical space and, more important, within her Social Space – is the catalyst that gives her access to the spiritual world that transformed her life amid her suffering and pending end of life.

Whether objectively there "really is" a transcendent, spiritual reality does not matter. What matters is that to this suffering woman the transcendent, spiritual reality is inspiringly real! So real, that it elevated her last moments into something sublime. (Or, in Frankl's view, she discovered Meaning for her life.)

For this woman, Transcendence is achieved by a focused use of the choices still available to her. They move her mental life in a particular direction. Through these choices she reaches out to, and allows herself to be embraced by an external, spiritual world. I repeat, whether that spiritual world "really" exists, in an objective sense, is irrelevant. What is relevant, what counts, is that to this dying woman the spiritual world is profoundly real. It is tangible; it is practical; it is immediate. For her, perhaps the most surprising development in her life is that she somehow found access to that spiritual world. As onlookers, we must acknowledge that it required an active decision, a choice, to accept the tree as the messenger from a spiritual world. It enlarged her world, so that she was able to transcend, in some way at least, the horrors of Auschwitz.

One of Frankl's themes is that we can find Meaning (I call it Transcendence) through our attitude toward unavoidable suffering. In the case of the dying woman, he demonstrates that it includes the impact of the raw environment on the individual plus the individual's response to that environment. The latter is all about one's choices. That even in a horrible context, such as Auschwitz, the individual does have a choice of how to respond. Thereby, one can discover meaning even in such a context. It can determine one's quality of life, even while dying.

A contrasting response to horrors among some inmates of concentration camps comes from the "Musselman" – the individual who had given up on life, who had renounced all connectedness to life beyond the camp, the antithesis of the young woman Frankl described. For the Musselman life in the camp had no Meaning – and no Transcendence. One would surely die very soon, even of one were in fairly good health. These inmates were "the walking dead." But unlike the young woman Frankl describes, the Muselmann's death was one of desolation, since he had already died before death.

Yet in Frankl's work the actual process of Transcendence – its component parts and processes – remains rather vague. One can easily fall into the trap of thinking that it involves mythical and extra-normal processes. I am convinced that we need not resort to mysticism to explain Transcendence.

As Frankl describes Transcendence, it ties in with my long research interest in understanding personal autonomy within social situations,[32] and links, the imprint from an external source that can color all component parts of a particular social situation.

Concerning autonomy, my starting thesis is that in every situation there exists some capacity for individuals to make choices, no matter what circumstances prevail. It may seem that this thesis contradicts common sense. The challenge is to discover and clarify just what choices are possible, or what local autonomy does, in fact, exist in seemingly controlled situations.

In a jail, does the prisoner have autonomy? Surely all his freedom to make choices is curtailed, which seems to contradict what I have said. The prisoner is forced to spend time in a particular place, is told with whom he can and cannot associate, where and when to sleep, what to eat, and so on. The controls over the prisoner's life seem all- pervasive. Yet listing the controls over the prisoner's life misses a crucial zone in which the prisoner has a great deal of autonomy – the freedom to be active, even to be inventive and creative.

The prisoner has the freedom to hate the confining authorities and to nurture that hatred, sometimes in elaborately creative ways producing a culture of resentment. Indeed, the very punitive controls of the prisoner's life by the prison administration – the manifold assaults on the prisoner's dignity – can help establish mental zones in which the prisoner's resentment is fostered and nurtured. By their actions prison authorities virtually plead with the prisoner: "Please hate us." They are issuing an invitation for creative responses focused on resentment and hatred. Physically a prisoner may be shackled. Yet his mind may gyrate violently. And, in unison with other, similarly situated prisoners, he can contribute to a culture of hatred for the authorities.

This is just one example of a prison where inmates are supposedly deprived of autonomy. Yet the situation contains zones where autonomy can exist. The real issue is how is the autonomy exercised. Think of Nelson Mandela, in prison for many years in South Africa. He refuses the lure to be consumed by hatred. Instead, he maintains an active, inner freedom that connects him to his vision of political and social freedom for South Africa's Black people. Although, at the time that freedom was largely imaginary, it was something very tangible in the Social Space active in his mind. It is what I have been calling External Autonomy – where an external reality – be it imaginary or not – becomes a factor in the here and now.

This is very similar to a situation reported by Viktor Frankl about his own life at Auschwitz. At one period he experienced almost unbearable pain in his foot. In response he turned his thoughts to giving a scholarly lecture to an academic audience as he had done before he came to Auschwitz and as he hoped to do again afterward. That world suddenly became so real and powerful that it wiped out the suffering and pain he was experiencing. It imported another context into his present situation. His Auschwitz situation is transcended by the intrusion of an external reality. He was exercising "external" autonomy, namely mentally living and participating in a world outside the one in which he physically lived. At the same time he renounced "internal" autonomy by not attending to some features of the world in which he actually existed at the time, such as the pain in his foot.

All this brings me back to the young woman, dying at Auschwitz. She, too, embraces an external world – to be sure, it is imaginary (as was Mandela's) – and brings it into her here and now. She is exercising a form of "external" autonomy while in a situation of extremely oppressive circumstances. This enables her to transcend much of the immediacy in which she exists. Stated differently, the link to an external, spiritual world produced an imprint on her present situation.

A very different scenario comes from the Musselman phenomenon. In some concentration camps there were individuals who had apparently given up on life, who walked around like zombies, destined to die very soon. But it would be a mistake to assume that these individuals operated without autonomy. They had merely renounced external autonomy. In their mindset, no life outside of the camp held any active meaning or relevance to their here and now. Instead, they exclusively concentrated on "internal" autonomy – dwelling on their current situation, with its pain and suffering, that extinguished their external autonomy altogether.

Concretely, as the Musselman's pain became unbearable, it left only one kind of autonomy, the active abandonment of life. This, too, included an exercise of autonomy. It did so in the form of one final decision: To abandon one's life to whatever assaults came. It was an affirmation of death. It was all-pervasive, affecting every act that touched their present life. To an observer, it seemed that mental rigor mortis had set in even before death had taken place. But to the Musselman this might not be true. One might have a richly focused inner life in the remaining days of one's existence. Perhaps it centered on celebrating one's death – "living it" to the fullest. Internal autonomy – in the form of total acceptance of a brutal Social Space – was exacting its final price, the extinguishing of life, even beyond its physical dimension.

This demonstrates, even more, the bearing of different uses of autonomy within a Social Space. When focused on external autonomy, as in the case of the young woman at Auschwitz, it can produce transcendence of a most horrifying situation – even if only temporarily. By contrast, focus on internal autonomy, when active in a horrifying situation, can augment the horrors. It is transcendence denied.

Benign Transcended Space: Why do we praise God while coping with extreme sickness, death and misfortune? To achieve Transcendence. We often do so, nurtured by a Social Space.

(1) A Manifestation – behavior

While taking part in Jewish religious services I have often wondered why we devote to so much effort to praising God. Christians and Muslims doubtless also devote much effort to the praise of God – Muslims' declaration that Allah is Great immediately comes to mind, as do Christian adorations of Jesus Christ. But I am particularly aware of it in prayers of my fellow Jews. On a typical Sabbath, our prayers practically gush in praise of God. It seems that we cannot find enough exemplary things to say about God, not enough adjectives to describe the praiseworthiness, glories, and grandeur of God. Even the prayer of mourning, the Kaddish, begins with "Magnified and sanctified be the name of God" and includes "Exalted and honored be the name of the Holy One."

(2) A manifestation – a social space that sponsors highly personal transcendence

The Kaddish prayer teaches us something, not only about how Jews address mourning, but an example of how societies can institutionalize Transcendence for its members. To get us started, first about the specifics of the Kaddish prayer: It takes place at the time of bereavement and anniversaries of the death of a loved one. It is said amid a congregation – not alone – and it is chanted in a specific stage within a religious service.

Within that service, it is chanted aloud, at a precise point in the service. The mourner stands – either alone or alongside others who may wish to join – in saying the Kaddish.

The Kaddish provides the mourner a context for experiencing his memory and relationship to the deceased person. It does this in a public forum yet in an entirely private format. The Kaddish prayer does not mention death, or bereavement, or even the name of the loved one. Instead, it is a buttressing ritual for the individual to form one's own content – of feelings and memories and emotions – that is not publicly announced and shared. I repeat, the public wording of the Kaddish prayer merely provides the outer wall within which the individual experiences one's particular way of transcending the present, with his own version of intimacy with the departed individual. These are not publicly shared. They take place in a socially guaranteed sacred space.

I learned this in an unexpected way. On a number of occasions I innocently thought that, after a religious service, I could talk to the person who had chanted the Kaddish and ask about their departed loved one. Each time I did so I was met with polite reluctance to talk. It finally dawned on me that I was intruding into their sacred space – and they were not about to violate that sacred space containing their private world of reliving their relationship to the loved one.

In short, the Jewish Kaddish prayer is an example of socially sponsored Transcendence via a particular Social Space. Other religions have their own versions of sponsored ways of mourning and remembrance. Here, I merely want to illustrate that a Social Space can be created in the service of particular objectives. In this case, it was a way to "structure" bereavement amid addressing both a community's concerns for social solidarity and continuity and an issue of intense personal privacy.

In a broader sense, when it comes to transcendence in a religious sense, we are in partnership with God. What God's actual attributes are we cannot know. But we do know that we can attribute transcendent attributes to God. We can attempt to have access to the God having such attributes. We can then come to have a measure of proximity and access to a transcendent space which may help us cope with issues in our own life. In all of this we are God's partners precisely through acknowledging God's vastly superior transcendence.[33]

Finally, a word about how transcended space might actually be experienced, how it feels. Perhaps it is a sublime sense of freedom. Here is a report by a passenger in a plane at the moment its pilot abruptly took extreme evasive action to prevent a possible collision with another plane. The passenger, not knowing why the plane suddenly appeared to break apart, was fully convinced that he was about to die. He states: "My life, past, present and future, was suddenly hysterically irrelevant, and in a kind of eternity that can reside in a second, my past and future, my memories, my whole life was insanely and laughably absurd…Within the wonder, beauty, irony and absurdity of that momentary eternity was a kind of freedom I had never known. In facing the nothingness of death, I saw the irrelevance of the desires and goals and regrets that had defined my life -- and I got free of them, free of everything, absolutely free."[34]

Malignant Transcended Space:
The case of Cults sponsoring mass suicide

They are a Closed Moral World.
They are nurtured by a Social Space.
They are impervious to alternatives.

The Manifestation

In 1997, in the vicinity of San Diego, thirty-nine members of the Heaven's Gate cult committed suicide. They did so under the conviction that they were thereby achieving Ultimate transcendence – their grandest yearnings were now in their reach. Along the way they heard the "message" that they would be picked up by a space ship and transported to another universe. Extraterrestrial beings were going to come and take them to that other domain. If they did not show up, then another form of conveyance to the other domain would have to be found – such as leaving their earthly body – hence the mass suicide.

Given our upbringing, these beliefs seem entirely weird, to put it mildly. They suggest virtual insanity. Pure myth!

It turns out that we, who are not enraptured by the cult, have our own myths.
Imagine you are a visitor from another planet. Once you have learned to communicate with us, to understand what we are saying, how do you think you would react to our belief in a "soul" or "heaven" to which we may go after our death here on earth? We earthlings are comfortable with our beliefs, with our particular brand of mysticism and unverifiable notions, but are uncomfortable with others' beliefs and their "strange" content. But don't deceive yourself. We "sane" people have plenty of unverifiable notions.

Of course the cultists' belief in their pending space travel to another domain really is empirically groundless and impossible to verify – it is pure mysticism – as are some of our own beliefs and articles of faith.

In addition to our myths about our end of life, we have a distinct set of myths about the cultists: They are delusional, zombies, and woefully wrong-headed. Their adherents need to be avoided – so as not to contaminate us – they need of re-programming to bring them back to "normalcy."

Two pieces of our mythology about cults stand out – and prevail in our Social Space. First, we assume that participants in such mass suicides must be totally isolated from the rest of us. Otherwise they would not engage in such behavior. They are physically separate, without contact with the relatively sane, everyday world in which most of us live. Yet in San Diego the cultists had "outside" jobs. They were free to come and go from the compound where they lived. They had contact with the outside word. Through the Internet, they were in contact with a large number of people beyond their immediate San Diego neighbors. Psychologically, the

Heaven's Gate cultists may have lived in a separate word. But they were not physically isolated. At least, not totally.

Second, we assume that cultists who kill themselves in unison must, surely, be under the total control of a leader. They must be zombies, who no longer have any autonomy whatsoever. Surely they simply carry out the bidding of a crazed and usually unscrupulous guru who is their leader. We blame it all on that leader. A headline in the *Washington Post* (March 30, 1997) read: "Surrender of Self is the Key to Cult Life." The followers are no longer functioning human beings. They have totally given themselves to a leader.

Yet by all evidence the Heaven's Gate cultists did not act like zombies, devoid of any will of their own. They performed fairly complicated work assignments on the outside, for which they got paid and for which they earned respect. They carried themselves with dignity and even continued to uphold such standard American interests as love of cars and fashionable clothes. And, a former cult member tells us, there was much laughter, discussion and joy within their communal living. Popular analyses stubbornly ignore these facts while insisting on the doleful description of cult life as blindly obedient to a crazy leader and devoid of personal independence, dignity and satisfaction. Despite these indicators about the cultists' life, we stubbornly adhere to our myths about cults. We do so because we cannot conceive of a Social Space that contains such "contradictory" components.

In our zeal to picture the cultists as crazy, we concentrate on the "message" they were following. The Heaven's Gate cultists fully expected (as I mentioned before) to be picked up by a space ship and transported to another universe. Extraterrestrials were going to come here and bring them to that other domain. If they did not show up, then another form of conveyance would be found – such as leaving their earthly body. Given our upbringing, these beliefs seem weird, to put it mildly. They suggest virtual insanity.

But all this is beside the point. The real issue is not what people actually believe. It is not a matter of one belief being more valid than another. It is not a matter of whether one belief is right and the other belief is wrong. Nor, whether one belief is crazy and another belief is sane. The real issue is the human yearning for transcendence – for overcoming life's turbulence and uncertainties; for coming to terms with the death and suffering of loved ones; for the discovery of meaning for one's existence amid the trivia, pettiness, and actual pain of daily living. Many formal religions provide the Social Space for addressing all of these issues. They offer transcendence that takes one beyond the pain, sorrow, and uncertainties in which we often find ourselves. They supply vision of something beyond the here and now.

What applies to formal religions applies even more to cults and other mythical programs. They, too, claim to give answers to the most troubling questions that confront us. They do so by inviting members to participate in what seems to be a most wondrously effective, personal way. They accomplish it by a nurturing Social Space, where transcendence is the central theme, governing members' community's life. Here transcendence is not some distant dream. It is here and now – brought to fruition by one's own participation, alongside a community of like-minded individuals.

Participation is crucial. One's transcendence – one's salvation or whatever the cult calls it – is not simply handed to you. You earn it by your participation in the cult's program, by giving your property, your diligence, your energy, your self and finally, your life. What greater gift can you possibly give than your life? Donating your life, in the form of suicide, can be seen by cultists as the greatest gift one can give in return for the greatest reward one can imagine. All this is facilitated by the Social Space in which the cult operates.

The final mysticism we outsiders cling to is that no one could possibly do such a thing as taking part in mass suicide of one's own free will. The cultists must be operating under extreme duress – be it physical duress or brainwashed mental duress. I answer that this is a misinterpretation. It takes our own Social Space – with its prevailing values and perspective about life – and applies it to that of the cultists. But in their reality the cultists feel exceedingly free. They are convinced that they do, in fact, have a great deal of autonomy, even while going to their death in suicidal passion.

Our confusion springs from the notion that such people could not possibly have any autonomy, any freedom of choice, any capacity to make decisions on their own. This is a profound misunderstanding of how human autonomy actually works. Autonomy, by individuals, is actually an inherent part of most human relationships and contexts. I have been studying autonomy for many years.[35] I am convinced that people can have autonomy in the unlikeliest situations. Typically the issue is not whether people have autonomy, but what sort of autonomy they have. In the case of cults, we see distinct zones in which people have autonomy and exercise it to the fullest. They have considerable autonomy to demonstrate their commitment to the sublime cause the guru has set out before them. The cult leader is the catalyst, setting out the social format of where and how autonomy exists. But it is the member, the participating cultist, who then fills in the blanks with one's occupational skills, property, sexuality, and, finally, one's life. The cultist sees this as free, voluntary contribution – gladly donated to the grand cause.

For the cultist there is a sense of unmatched fulfillment and joy in the act of contributing to ultimate transcendence. That ultimate transcendence, that reaching of one's highest yearnings, is achieved here and now. One's own contribution has made it happen. What greater glory could there possibly be?

If we refuse to see the power of this seductive process, we will forever be surprised and shocked by cults. Each new cult – each new extremist movement – will again startle us, even as it exacts its terrible price.

What we must learn:
The cult phenomenon takes place within a nurturing Social Space. That Social Space has specified transcendence as the prevailing value and operationalized the process of implementing it.

Malignant Transcendent Space:
The case of Hitler: A false messiah

The false messiah claims to be the unique gatekeeper for entry into transcendent space. There Ultimates – the grandest objectives of life – can be reached, here and now. It will all materialize if you follow the messiah unquestioningly. Whatever he demands is holy writ. He, personally, guarantees its success.

Once this idea is embraced, it impassions people to follow all the "messiah's" directives. It opens up zones of behavior into which people will fling themselves with utmost fervor, believing that Ultimate objectives are in their grasp. It justifies every directive extolled by the "messiah," no matter how brutal and murderous.

The result can be a malignant form of transcendence – within a Social Space that nurtures that malignancy.

Manifestation

The advent of Adolf Hitler in Germany is remarkable in many ways. He was an Austrian by birth, not a German, who became Germany's leader. This man harnessed the German people's fears and aspirations in ways that made them willing to engage in deeds beyond comprehension, make sacrifices beyond compare, and adopt levels of self-deception that crossed the outer boundary of sanity, entering fully into the realm of the delusional.

Among the German citizens Hitler energized the disadvantaged, the destitute, and the disenchanted. He also electrified many of the comfortably well-off, the entrenched members of the country's privileged classes. He succeeded in polluting the thinking of people among whom were some of the most sophisticated and most educated people in the world. They joined Hitler in attempting to actualize a cosmic dream. They became his followers.

Hitler was regarded by most of these followers as a man of superhuman attributes, a man who would catapult Germany to its greatest destiny through his personal leadership. That leadership would restore, revitalize and activate Germany's dormant energy. It would bring forth Germany's rightful glory before which the entire world would stand in awe. On the individual German citizen, Hitler would bestow a sense of personal fulfillment and pride never before experienced. He would bring many fond wishes to fruition. He embodied and personified their innermost yearnings. In effect he was, to many, a messiah.

Therein lay Hitler's appeal, the foundation of his success, and the ultimate fraud of his mission. And therein, too, lies a lesson for all of us about the nature of the messiah phenomenon and the Social Space that nurtures it.

I shall discuss the nature of messiahs in a very secular way – without entering fully into the difference between, say, the Jewish and Christian perspectives on the messiah. I believe that Jews and Christians – although they operate in a different Social Space – are not as far apart on the messiah issue as one might think. Jews believe that the messiah, who is going to establish the ultimate rule of God on Earth, has not yet come. Human life is to be lived with such nobility and decency that the messiah is likely to come. For many Jews, it is the pursuit of the coming of the messiah, of being worthy of the messiah's coming, that constitutes a reason for living a good and decent life.

Christians believe the messiah, in the person of Jesus, has in fact already come. Through the example of his own life, Jesus pointed the way to the good and worthy life. This lesson is to be implanted in the religiously grounded life, one that is worthy of the example already set. Christian belief further holds that a second coming of Christ will happen to carry out much the same purpose envisioned by Jewish belief.

In a way both religions are urging their members to pursue a worthy and good life, with a messiah as a fundamentally personal moral guide, one through whom the ordinary mortal human being can find a personal way to transcend the mundane and enter into a tangible, realizable moral compact with a transcending moral universe. Personal salvation is facilitated through the messiah, be he postulated to come at some time in the future (in the Jewish view) or having already made an appearance on Earth (in the Christian view).

The "personal" side of the Judeo-Christian messiah vision has three components:

One, the messiah is a person who, through his or her own life, personifies a profound moral message. (The messiah differs from a prophet, who also has a profound moral message, but whose personal life does not necessarily personify and exemplify the moral message, nor does that personal life serve as a vehicle for redemptive effect in people's lives. I am referring to the Judeo-Christian view of a prophet. For Muslims the "prophet" Muhammed is regarded as the messiah.)

Two, the messiah's message is directed to the individual person – the citizen, the member of the community, the ordinary human being – in a very personal way, offering him or her a personal access to moral salvation, a personal attachment to sublime and ultimate moral grace.

Three, the individual, in response to the message from the messiah, is expected to act in his or her own life in a manner that connects to the messiah's demonstrated vision of the state of ultimate grace. Through one's actions, one thereby helps to actualize the messiah's wondrous vision. In short, the individual is not passive. Instead, one actively contributes, through one's own behavior, to transforming the messiah's vision into concrete reality. One does so by actively embracing and helping to enact the messiah's vision.

A messiah is a leader. Hence, a word about leaders and the nature of leadership. The difference between an actual leader and a delusional "leader" (who is apt to be a patient in a psychiatric facility) may chiefly be that one has followers and the other does not. Leaders require followers who believe them. The followers attribute leadership qualities to the leader and legitimize leadership by their willingness to follow. Without followers, there is no leader. Those who imagine themselves to be leaders but lack anyone to believe them may eventually end up in a psychiatric facility. They are thought to be living in an unreal world. The "real" world is likely to consign them to a facility in which their "unreality" is granted a limited and highly circumscribed right to exist. Their "leadership" can be enacted as a permitted illusion in a hospital facility, but nowhere else.

In the "real" world, leadership is made up of a social compact between leader and followers. It may be explicit or implicit. But it is nonetheless a compact, an "agreement" that specifies the constraints on each party to the compact. It also specifies the kind and range of freedom for each party. Each has a particular zone of behavior in which it can operate rather freely but beyond which it cannot go. And, most important, each derives distinctive benefits from the relationships.

This code is glaringly evident when we deal with messianic leaders, individuals who exercise leadership on the basis of supposedly extraordinary attributes. Hitler was one of these. His "extraordinary attributes" were constantly on display.

Germany suffered a disastrous loss in the 1914-1918 World War I. That war was followed by the humiliating Treaty of Versailles, in which Germany was heavily penalized. The aftermath saw economic turmoil culminating in the catastrophic rate of inflation in the 1920s. Hitler drew on this despoiling and losses, emphasizing over and over again how unfairly Germany was being treated by her supposed enemies – internal ones (i.e., Jews) as well as external ones. He would come to the rescue. He would return Germany to its rightful place, its glorious role in history.

Hitler was a spellbinding speaker, and he made ample use of this ability. Beginning in the 1920s, in speech after speech, and in place after place, he hammered away at Germany's losses and deprivations from World War I, and how he would see to it that these would be rectified. Germany's true and rightful glory would be restored. Her honor would be returned. Her economic house would be put in order. Her political power would be regained, and her military strength once more placed in a state of pre-eminence among the powers of the world. Her racial purity would be protected and enhanced. He personally would see to it that these things would get done. He vouched for it.

The Germans believed Hitler. The vast majority fell under his spell. Here was a man who "really understood" their secret, innermost fears and yearnings – so they thought. They believed that he was in touch with something that concerned them profoundly. As a result they were prepared to entrust their destiny to him. They accepted his entire package of proposed programs, those they could understand and those they could not understand; those with which they agreed and those with which they did not agree. In 1933, they elected Hitler to head the German government.

Once in office, Hitler continued his messianic style of leadership. He and his disciples proclaimed the he, above all, personified Germany's destiny. He stood between Germany and her enemies. He could see into the future. He we would ennoble Germany and its people. All this was promoted and implemented in what may have been the most intense propaganda campaign of hero worship the world has ever seen.

The propaganda machine was immensely successful. A large number of people – surely a majority of the citizens of Germany – believed the propaganda, the speeches, and the exhortations emanating from the Nazi regime. It seemingly, masterfully, operated in a transcended space.

It is crucial that one realizes that the propaganda was not one-sided: It was not addressed to a passive citizenry, one that simply accepted what it was told. On the contrary, the citizenry was active. They attributed superhuman vision to Hitler. They put this into practice by believing him even when he told the most outrageous lies, and they followed him even when he led them into the most disastrous and lethal exploits. They attributed to Hitler supreme sensitivity to Germany's most fundamental destiny and honor. They attributed to Hitler capacities that ordinary mortals simply do not have. They did the dirty work to help bring his most deranged dreams into existence – such as participating in the murder of millions of innocent people who, supposedly, "detracted" from the "purity" of their race. Hitler, they believed, personified and made concrete the ultimate destiny of the German people. Virtually all Germans – the educated and the uneducated, the lowly under classes and the upper classes – came to believe in him as Germany's savior, its messiah.

To the individual German, Hitler's specific directives might at times seem drastic, harsh, and difficult to understand. But those directives were invariably regarded as holy writ, as emanating from a leader whose vision went beyond what ordinary mortals can see and comprehend. He was regarded as no ordinary mortal. His messages were regarded as sacred and were treated as such.

Hitler's followers demonstrated their faith in Hitler-as-messiah not just with intoxicated swooning and roars of approval while listening to his speeches. They translated their faith into deeds – ranging from passivity when innocent victims of Nazism were persecuted all the way to actively participating in and contributing to such programs. It included willingly participating in Hitler's military adventurisms, where their sons were likely to be sacrificed. Hitler was granted infallibility. This, I reiterate, requires followers who actively grant this ability – who believe that the leader rightfully and actually has this ability. It is not merely a matter of a leader claiming to have this ability. The followers grant the leader the right to act totally capriciously and arbitrarily, without having to be accountable for actions. This is part of the social compact between leader and followers.

In that compact the followers retain freedom in a specific zone within which they can exercise autonomy. But autonomy exists only in that zone, resulting in a particular kind of behavior. It is absent from other zones. Specifically, the followers – the German citizens, in this case – have the autonomy to create ways of venerating their messiah and the cause he has personally set out for them. This encompasses donating their personal belongings, enthusiasms and energy, skills and capacities for performing work, and professional expertise, up to and including donating their lives. All this is done in the service of the grand cause set before them. It is often done joyfully, with the sense that one is contributing to the most noble venture, to the ultimate destiny of one's country and person. Hitler was perceived to bring the ultimate destiny up close so that, by serving him, one had the unique opportunity to personally contribute to actualizing that ultimate reality. One had the once-in-a-lifetime opportunity to participate in the very highest form of salvation – for one's country and for one's self. In short, one is intoxicatingly immersed in transcended space.

Yet the autonomy of followers is strictly limited. There are zones of behavior in which the follower may not exercise autonomy at all. Most notably, one is not permitted to question the sanctity (and sanity) of the leader. One could not question Hitler's judgment. One could not argue against any Nazi directives that bore the imprimatur of Hitler's personal order. It would amount to leaving the transcended, sacred space. Perhaps the most frightening example, in all of human history, is the following:

What may be the most murderous directive of all time – the "Final Solution" to exterminate all Jews – was said to have been ordered by Hitler personally. Yet it was apparently never written down and signed. Nor do we have an authenticated, witnessed, and verified statement that he ever gave that monstrous order verbally. The "order," so profound in its impact on the fate of millions of human individuals, remains entirely murky. This, surely, is the ultimate acceptance of the messianic leader's exemption from accountability. Any opposition was deemed a deadly sin, a vile form of moral transgression – and treated accordingly by Nazi authorities. (The old debate over obedience to authority – that Germans were forced to obey Hitler's Nazism – misses the point. Obedience to Hitler was regarded as a moral imperative, something far more powerful than the physical force behind it. Disobedience was unthinkable – and many former Nazi officials said so.)

Hitler, the messiah, also operated within constraints, within particular zones of autonomy. He had to perform miracles, and continue to do so – hence his frantic turning to ever more daring and more questionable enterprises. By contrast, non-daring routines were rejected as dreary. They might have contributed to disenchantment, to de-mystifying this messiah. Enchantment must be nurtured through miraculous, non-routine, extraordinary deeds – such as Hitler's commanding Germany to wage war simultaneously against all the greatest powers of his era (Great Britain, France, the Soviet Union and the United States) under the most adverse circumstances. The latter included launching a land war against the Society Union, with its vast snow-laden regions and winter blizzards. Hitler began that war during summer, fantasizing the Germany would win before winter came. But even if winter did come before full victory,

Germany would surely prevail! (Even though his soldiers did not have winter clothing.)

Here we have a cosmic joke. The Hitler who undertook such grotesque ventures could only do so if he actually believed his own fantasies. He no longer merely tried to deceive others. He had reached the point of deceiving himself. Here, it seems, the grandiose deceptions had reached their final destiny, the deceiver himself.

The messianic leader has the autonomy to create out-of-ordinary happenings while, at the same time, shunning dreariness and the merely ordinary. In the latter sphere, he decidedly lacks autonomy, the capacity to participate and engage himself. The messiahs of the word must shun routines that reveal their own foibles and shortcomings as ordinary mortal human beings. By definition, they are beyond the ordinary. This illusion is best done by maintaining social distance from ordinary, day-to-day human interactions. Such distance enables the followers to assign extraordinary attributes to the messiah. This is further nurtured when the life span of the messiah is short and the messiah dies a martyr to the cause he has espoused. Here, of course, the lives of Jesus and Martin Luther King Jr., come to mind. Both lived short lives, leaving a legacy that followers were free to amplify and elaborate. Much of the lore of messiahship is in the hands of followers – and even more so after the death of the messiah. Then the followers have virtually unlimited freedom to invent, or at least exaggerate, extraordinary attributes and miraculous deeds by their messiah.

In many ways, messiahs are alike. Yet as the lives of Jesus and Martin Luther King Jr. illustrate, there surely is a world of difference between such exemplary, morally righteous individuals and the sort of messiahship demonstrated by Hitler. It is the difference between the true messiah and the false messiah. The true messiah personifies and exemplifies in his or her life the highest values of a human community. The false messiah, on the other hand, manages to attach some of the highest values to him- or herself, but in the final analysis tramples on these values, destroying their viability rather than honoring them.

In the case of Hitler, this included desecrating the yearning for national community in Germany by creating monstrous disrespect for German communal life; replacing the German yearning for economic and political tranquility with the most profound economic and political dislocation; converting legitimate pride in the German people's accomplishments into the most vicious form of racism and jingoistic nationalism.

One reason why the false messiah is often so very hard to expose is because the followers are actively and personally involved in the messianic process. They derive a sense of personal empowerment from the messiah's message, mostly because they become heavily engaged in the process of carrying out the messianic message. They are part of the process – what I have been calling the third component of messiahship. Namely, the individual follower's contribution to making the process work. That individual follower's contribution is very likely to include rationalizations that attest to the supposed truth of the false messiah's message and help carry that message forward. It is a crucial part of their life in transcended space.

Hence when a German citizen became a functionary in the SS – helping to implement the persecution of innocent victims of the crazed Nazi policy – he buttressed that participation with all sorts of personally satisfying rationalization as to why this was really necessary. Individuals invented reasons to justify their particular contribution. The Nazi cause became a personal cause which, they believed, was morally justified. The followers thereby contributed much of the moral underpinnings for perpetuating Hitler's program. To be sure, theirs was a very circumscribed and limited zone of personal autonomy. It supported Hitler and refused to countenance any criticism. It underwrote the Nazis program. It helped create and nurture this false messiah. I repeat, much of the followers' personal autonomy was used to create the rationalizations – the justifying myths – that supported the Nazi program of horror.

I am reminded of Dr. Eduard Wirths.[36] He was a Christian physician who began as a very humane, caring and courageous doctor who, in the 1930s, continued to treat Jewish patients, often secretly. At that time this was an increasingly unpopular and risky thing for a Christian physician to do. Yet this same physician eventually became a major contributor to the extermination program at Auschwitz. He devised the "selections" – deciding who would die right away and who would live a little longer – administered by physicians when the hapless victims arrived at Auschwitz. To justify his contribution to the program of horror at Auschwitz Dr. Wirths wrote passionate love letters to his wife. In these letters he states that he is involved in horrendous activities. But it is all worth while because, he feels, it will lead to a better future for their family and, in particular, for their children. With the love of his family in his heart, he could go through with the horrors.

Such is the art of rationalization that helped underwrite participation in horrors by an individual who started out as an unusually sensitive, humane and courageous person. Rationalization is a way to convert the vision of the future, cultivated by a false messiah, into a course of action in the immediate world in which people lead their daily lives. The followers believe that the messiah gives access to their ultimate destiny – their personal salvation. Perceiving tangible access to that salvation – surely the greatest gift one can imagine – many followers gladly donate their lives as they engage in deeds that are utterly despicable from any moral point of view, even their own. Yet followers benefit. They are convinced that they attain personal access to ultimate values – a form of salvation – through this course of action.

What are the benefits for the messianic leader? What does one derive from the contribution of one's followers? Validation for leadership. Without it the leadership would be an empty shell, subject to rejection by the "sane" world. Concrete validation of the leader's calling buttresses one against the doubters and nonbelievers. It augments one's own efforts and provides an apparent reality test of one's purpose and mission in life. One can believe that one really is the messiah.

The lesson for all of us is that messiahs – true messiahs and false messiahs – can awaken our innermost yearnings by providing a glimpse of ultimate moral values and do so in a form that makes these values seem attainable here and now, through our own actions, in the social space in which we find ourselves.

The messianic process – consisting of the role of the messiah and the role of followers – can create a social space. In it transcendence – be it true or false, actual or imagined – is the unifying theme that makes it operate.

This teaches us that transcendence – this dream of access to the ultimate – can be the catalyst in the formation of a particular kind of social space. I will suggest that there are also other kinds of social space. But this does not diminish the importance of this kind of social space.

Postscript: The Bi-Polarity of the Ultimate

Access to the Ulimate has been a theme of this discussion. It can produce empowering transcendence in the life of the individual and the actions of a community. But access to the Ultimate includes a second dimension, amounting to bi-polarity. Namely, that in addition to empowerment, access to the Ultimate can produce extraordinary vulnerability, including limitless pain and disorientation, a seeming rupture of the core of one's being. This was brought home to me after many Muslims responded with the most profound pain and rage to a denigrating cartoon of the Prophet Muhammad in a Western newspaper. They interpreted it as desecration of something altogether sacred.

Desecration of the sacred – this is the key. The sacred identifies the Ultimate – the Ultimate articles of faith about one's destiny, about one's reason for being, about the moral core of one's existence, about one's very identity as a person. Desecrating a sacred object means, in the mind the observant individual, that one's very existence has been besmirched in a most horrifying way. Not surprisingly, during the Iraq war Muslims reacted with rage upon hearing that a page from the Koran was allegedly flushed down a toilet. Their reaction was a response to desecration of something sacred.

Let me give you two examples from my own life. They illustrate, I think, the deep impact of besmirched sacred symbols – even to a rather secular person.

I was born into an Orthodox Jewish family in a small village in southern Germany. I left at the age of eleven through a child-rescue operation, the "Kindertransport" launched from England. My parents and older brother could not escape and did not survive the Holocaust. In 1979, forty years after my departure, I visited the village, my birthplace. I was no longer an "Orthodox" Jews. In fact, for many years I had not participated in formal Jewish practices, or religiosity of any kind. Recently, however, I had returned to a Jewish affiliation and observed some Jewish religious practices.

In the village I was received very warmly. I was able to go, and did go, anywhere I wanted, including entering the house where I was born. There was only one place I was unable to enter. It was the synagogue. It was now a bank. I stood in front of it. Frozen. Unable to move.

This, to me, was the second desecration of my synagogue – where I had stood next to my father in prayer, where I knew each congregant, each chant, each communal celebration of our religious life. The synagogue was a sacred place. Now it was a bank.

The first desecration had taken place during the *Kristallnacht* pogrom against Jews in November 1938. During that night the sacred Torah scrolls had been dragged out of our synagogue and thrown onto piles of manure. The memory of this desecration of the Torah scrolls was as painful to me – then, and now, this many years later – as the murder of my parents and my brother. It has not left me. It shattered a part of my mental world.

It taught me about the impact of desecration of a sacred object.

In conclusion, our access to the Ultimate introduces us to a profound bi-polarity. One the one hand, it brings empowerment because it helps us go beyond the limitations and encumbrances in our daily life. It does so by bringing transcendence into our immediate daily life. It thereby brings a sense of profound meaning to our personal identity. On the other hand, when the transcended world is, somehow, desecrated – when the Ultimate is besmirched – transcendence can once again enter our immediate, daily life. Now it does so in a form that seems to fracture and shatter our mental world, as our identity is being destroyed.

Both polarities are part of the human condition. It is enacted in Social Space when that space is permeated by the transcendence phenomenon.

Another example of Bi-Polarity:
The case of religious zealotry. A brief note --

Social Space is sometimes permeated by religion. And there, too, Ultimates can exist in bi-polar form.

Religions are very much concerned with delineating Ultimates – of trying to fathom life's deepest meaning amid major transitions and occurrences while we are alive. This includes, among many things, confronting life's ending, as in sorrows and bereavement, as well as life's beginnings and exuberances, as in celebrating births and marriage. Typically, religions provide responses to such issues, giving their adherents anchorage amid the ups and downs of daily living. The actual responses which a religion offers tend to become enshrined in orthodoxies that can attain a firm status, becoming powerful ingredients of a community's religion-based existence. These can claim to be its Ultimates – to be worshipped and defended with zeal. They can be nurtured in Social Space, which specifies how the Ultimates are actually part of daily living by members of the community.

When I wrote these words Westerners were aghast upon hearing – and thanks to modern technology, seeing – public beheadings and other forms of grotesque cruelty we believed had long ago been eliminated from the repertoire of human social behavior. Yet here it was, coming to us in the form of ISIS practices in the Middle East – with its claim of adhering to Ultimate religious orthodoxy. In our time, it was happening. In our time, it was brought to our reluctant attention. To be sure we have our own history, and heritage, of grotesque cruelty. Remember the trench warfare of the First World War, where thousands of innocent young men hacked one another to death on many a single day. When each side claimed that

God was on its side. And when, thanks to Bob Dylan, we are reminded that when God is on your side, you don't have to count the dead – even when their number defies counting.

Still, there is something in the recent CELEBRATION of cruelty that goes beyond the previous horrors. It takes us back to the joy-filled celebration of mass burning of witches during the 30 Years War in the 1600s. There, amid zealotry around that religious war, innocent people might quickly meet a horrendous fate, publicly feted, after being accused of some sort of religious transgression. Is religious fervor – with its supposed access to Ultimates – especially susceptible to communal zealotry? Is the zealotry a result to a perceived threat to a community's religion-based existence?

Religious fervor can be nurtured in a Social Space where, in the form of prominently displayed religious symbols, awareness of Ultimates can be in constant view. The bi-polarity of Ultimates is on display when the Ultimates are deemed to have been besmirched and purified through zealous assertion of religious rectitude. These can take the form of acts of incredible cruelty, all nurtured in a Social Space. Not a pretty picture of the bi-polarity of religiosity, or of the supposed sacred bonds that bind a community.

MEANINGFUL SPACE:

The Creation of Meaning Phenomenon

We humans expect.
We humans remember.
We humans think.
We humans believe.

What do these mental processes have in common?
They create meaningful social space. They do so by bringing into that space things from the past and things from the future, things from the real and things from the imagined, things from afar and things from nearby. The result is a *concrescence* (*), a coming together, that creates a new, meaningful reality for the persons inhabiting a Social Space. And this new meaningful reality can produce *emanations*, giving rise to new meanings, including drastic change of meaning in another Social Space.

(*) The concept *concrescence* was developed by the philosopher / mathematician Alfred North Whitehead.

This chapter is about how Social Space creates and nurtures meanings. And also how Social Space can store, activate, and dissipate meanings.

The following begins with an imaginary story about a transaction in a shoe store. It mentions sex but is not about sex. It is about concrescence that creates meaning in a Social Space. I have previously used this story to focus on how very different social contexts can impinge on one another through what I called the Rider phenomenon – namely, how items from an "outside" context make an imprint on a local context. Here, by contrast, I use this story to recognize how different kinds of Meaning are created in Social Space, where concrescence is the vehicle that makes it happen.

Silent but real Meaning – (1)

A woman goes into shoe store. A salesman waits on her. She tries on a pair of shoes. The salesman says: "These shoes look very good on you." The woman vaguely senses that a male says these words, that a man speaks approvingly of how she looks in the shoes she is now putting on her feet. That male approval may be the catalyst that will sway her decision to buy the shoes.

In this situation sex is not openly mentioned at all. Yet the customer and salesman may both be sensitive to sexual nuances. The woman may believe that male approval of how she looks in the shoes indicates her heterosexual attractiveness. The salesman may believe that a hint of sexuality, mentioning the woman's attractiveness from his masculine perspective, might foster a successful sale; perhaps his masculinity is invested in being a successful salesman to women.

Here sex is intruding into a non-sexual business transaction – the evaluation and possible purchase of a pair of shoes. But it does so in the form of silent meaning. Despite not being openly mentioned, sex may be the catalyst that swings the transaction toward a particular conclusion. In short, in this shoe store example sexuality is part of the concrescence of meaning that underwrites the purchase of a pair of shoes.

In a moment I shall illustrate the concrescence phenomenon from quite a different perspective. But first, let us consider the imaginary shoe store events a bit further.

Loud, no longer silent, Meaning – (2)

Suppose the salesman thinks that the woman's response to him is a bit flirtatious. He may take this as evidence of sexual encouragement. He responds with more blatant allusions to sex and eventually escalates the sexual banter, suggesting that the woman join him in the back storeroom for a more explicit sex transaction.

What are the woman's options in this situation – where the benefit of silent sexual meaning is abandoned, replaced by open airing of sexual meaning? She might slap the salesman. She might report him to the store manager. She might abruptly walk out of the store. Or she might accept the salesman's offer, either joining him in the storeroom for a sex tryst or, at least, give serious thought to doing so.

Why might she even consider the last two options?

Let us suppose that before she left home that morning, the woman had another of her rather frequent verbal fights with her husband. She has been married to him for several years. Before their marriage and even during the early years of the marriage, she had many a dream of how her husband's and her life together would evolve beautifully – the many things they would do together, the joys they would experience by being each other's best friend as well as romantic lover.

During this morning's fight with her husband the woman was reminded once again that her dreams of married life with her husband had never come true. Most of all, she felt that her husband had never lived up to his promises. That he failed her over and over again. In the early years of their marriage she had overlooked her husband's failings. But they kept happening, again and again. In short, the meaning of her married life was under assault.

Her world of dreams of what marriage might have been intruded and permeated much of her sex life with her husband. It made a debilitating imprint. During sexual moments with her husband she could never shake off the sense of profound disillusionment with him and the reality it created for her and their marriage. These thoughts were guests in their bedroom. They made sex with her husband a joyless and sometimes unpleasant activity. In short, sex with her husband had very ambivalent meaning.

This background led to her being responsive to the salesman, a total stranger, someone she would never see again, someone she would not introduce to her circle of friends.

How would sex with the salesman, this stranger, differ from sex with her husband? Surely the physiology of sex would be very little different. Yet sex with the stranger holds a promise of having entirely different meaning. It would be a brief but gloriously fulfilling event. Why? With this stranger, sex – whether it actually happens or is merely imagined – would carry none of the ambivalent meaning of sex with her husband. It would be free of its many disillusions and disappointments. It would be free of the unhappiness associated with her husband's failings that had been inflicted on her and carried over to her sexuality with her husband.

You may ask, is sex with the stranger free of meanings? Not at all. This new sex, this promise of a fling, invites distinctive kinds of meanings. Whether it is carried out or merely contemplated, it is permeated by fantasy of what sex could be. The woman promises herself that she will never see the salesman again. There will be no souring reality test. Hence, sex with him can land her squarely in her fantasyland. For once in her life, fantasy will prevail. Sex will consist of pure joy, pure freedom, pure creativity, pure uncontaminated lust, and more. It is sex drenched in fantasy, implementing its dreams.

Emanating Meanings – (3)

Let us assume that the woman actually had a sexual fling with the salesman. And through it, she actually experienced some of her dreamed-of sexuality. This sex experience may then emanate, creating new meaning for sex with her husband. As a result, out of a sense of betrayal and guilt, the woman may suddenly become far more ardent in her sexual behavior with her husband – much to his surprise. Or, she may now totally renounce sexual activity with the husband – "Whatever did I see in him?"—refusing to make further compromises in the marriage. Both of these could be exported emanations from her new-found sexual thrills.

Other spheres of Meaning

The process of creating meaning exists in many spheres of human behavior – not only in the sphere of sex. It exists in such valued spheres as eating, drinking, fighting wars, career activities, religiosity, making money, family-focused living, to mention just a few. Each sphere has distinct focus and function in our life. And each can be the space where concrescence of external influences takes place, and creates distinct meanings.

As an example, let us consider eating. The focus is not on the physiology, the dietary aspect, or even the nutritional aspect of eating. Instead, focus will be on the socially institutionalized format of eating. The resulting culture of eating is evident in everyday patterns of how people eat meals and how they do so amid the creation of meaning.

Families tend to develop their own culture of eating meals. Here is one such pattern: Family members regularly sit down for dinner together. It is a fundamental ritual in their lives. Here face-to-face interactions can be nurtured (or infuriatingly strained) among family members. Information is shared and evaluated. Values are brought out into the open. It is a time and place where family solidarity is actively practiced.

On the other hand, many a modern family has little time for family sit-down dinners. Eating frequently takes place individually, or with colleagues, or on the run, or in quick trips to restaurants. In each of these a very different culture is in play.

In each culture distinctive meanings permeate eating. In the case of the on-the-run eating habits, the rush of modernity permeates and prevails. On weekdays many of us don't have time for leisurely and lengthy family dinners. Our careers set the tempo and focus of our priorities. Having meals with family may be quite low on the list of personal priorities.

In the family-sit-down dinners, on the other hand, ethnic, religious, and family history meanings are brought into the immediate present. These are kept alive through the regular enactment of rituals around the dinner table. A prayer before the meal, to cite just one ritual, is apt to be the carrier of family customs via the ways of how the prayer is said – sung or spoken, loudly or softly, short or long, fixed word content or improvised, and so on – in compliance with "how it is always done in our family." Here family continuity is a permeating meaning. It is derived from the wider world of one's family history, one's relatives, as well as specific family experiences – including particular prayers said during significant family events, such as at a birth or death in the family.

When it comes to meals, ethnic groups differ greatly in how meals and other forms of eating are permeated by meanings. One could dwell on the Jewish culture (which I happen to know best), where eating is valued as a focus of family life, as a crutch in time of stress and illness, and as an element of religious life, notably Kosher food prescriptions. Concerning the management of stress and illness, the proverbial mother's chicken soup comes to mind. With it, the crusading mother comes to the rescue at times of illness and stress. Despair and fear will be dispelled. A new meaning will prevail. You will get well, your mother and her chicken soup will guarantee it!

Let us turn to the creation of meaning in a very different context: Consider a British custom of meeting many a crisis with the response: *"Let us sit down and have a cup of tea."* If nothing else, this can provide a momentary breathing space that eliminates overly hasty responses to a crisis. It can create a focus on reason, a culture of deliberation and balanced weighing of issues and, even, a potential for friendship – all activated amid a crisis that may have erupted over conflicting interests between individuals who are now confronting each other. The elaborate, mannered decorum of tea drinking – pouring the tea from a pot, assuring just the right temperature, adding the appropriate amount of milk – further connects the tea drinking ceremony to other zones of meaningful "civilized" communal living. The mannered tea drinking also relates to other areas of life, reminding the participants in no uncertain terms that a wider reality is relevant and bearing on their immediate, present concerns. In turn, this precisely orchestrated interaction can originate new meaning in other spheres of life in which the participating actors are engaged. For example, the tea drinking ceremony may induce some civility into other such spheres.

What I have just said about meaning in the British tea drinking custom could be applied to the culture of drinking in pubs in Ireland. Here the sociability of drinking is open to many facets of one's life. In the pub, what one talks about, sings about, cries about while drinking brings all of these together – into concrescence of meaningful living moments. And even more, the pub can be a shunting station. Its meanings can be exported. What you have experienced in the pub may stay with you when you go home, when you go to work, when you are awake and when you are asleep. And when you dream. You will surely go back to the pub – where your life's many meanings can be safely explored and celebrated.

Producing meaning on a large scale:

A previous chapter discussed creation of meaning in a very large context, namely the situation in Hitler's Germany. There, Hitler deliberately created and drove home the myth of Germany's shame for having been "unjustly" punished after World War I. He used it to permeate German thought so thoroughly, fostering such national rage, that it granted him the freedom to sponsor horrendous deeds in the name of washing away Germany's shame. It created a mindset that justified, to Germans, taking part in actions of unlimited ferocity – such as genocide and another World War. Here, surely, we see that meanings have consequences, especially when they permeate the social space of an entire country.

In short, meaning can be generated on a large scale. In the United States, at the moment of this writing, in the year 2016 – after the election of Donald Trump as president – we see the makings of new, large-scale meaning. At this time it is unclear what the meaning will be.

Silent Meaning Again:

There are many forms of silent meaning behavior, in addition to the imaginary one I mentioned earlier. Here are examples.

(1) The case of a wily lady

I am reminded of Indira Ghandi's first visit to the United States and the Soviet Union after she became India's prime minister, when she requested badly needed economic aid for her country. No one could accuse Mrs. Ghandi of sexually flirting with the leaders of these countries. But her manner was so charming, so sexually tinged, that President Lyndon Johnson proclaimed that he would give her anything she wanted. The usually dour Aleksey Kosygin, the Soviet premier, was temporarily transformed into an animated, gracious host. Both, Johnson and Kosygin, produced generous aid for India.

*(2)*A silent format: Again, the Kaddish prayer

Jews respond to death with a central prayer, the Kaddish, recited by close relatives of a deceased person. It is recited again and again, at stipulated times, to commemorate the deceased person's life and death. Typically, family members recite the Kaddish prayer on the anniversary of the death of each parent or sibling or child of their own. They do so during a religious service. They regard it as a sacred obligation, which touches the very core of their relationship to the deceased person, to their religion, if not to life itself.

Yet the Kaddish prayer does not mention death, or mourning or, even, the deceased individual for whom the prayer is being recited. Its statements are fixed, beginning with "Magnified and sanctified be the name of God," and continue in this vein, declaring the grandeur of God and His power to direct the course of human destiny and the yearning that this will lead, above all, to peace.

Astonishingly, in the Kaddish prayer none of the personal aspects of mourning is mentioned! The sense of loss, of remembering the person who has died – with whom ones has had a deep connection, who is likely to have affected one's own life in the most profound way, whose departure seems to wrench away a piece of one's very essence – none of this is mentioned!

Yet all such feelings are likely to be activated by this prayer, which does not mention these things but merely sets them in motion. The Kaddish is the mobilizing occasion in a specifically created Social Space for activating silent Meanings – which, during much of one's everyday living are apt to be dispersed and dormant. During the recitation of the Kaddish these meanings are active partners to the spoken prayer words. Perhaps most powerfully, the reciter of the Kaddish is not limited to mere verbal expressions. The Kaddish opens a zone of active grief that is not limited to some prescribed formulaic statement. Instead, *it opens up space for creating one's personal version of grief and remembrance.* But it does so in a silent but active format. Not only is the Kaddish chanted at a particular time within the religious service. It also has a precise ending of the grieving process! I discovered this rather surprising feature when, in my innocence, I occasionally spoke to a Kaddish chanter after the end of the service. I inquired about the deceased, trying to draw out the Kaddish sayer a little bit. I invariably found, despite a polite response, that the grieving process was decidedly over. There was not much readiness to talk about it. The grieving had taken place in a precisely defined silent space – a space that contained open territory but also definite boundaries.

Dormant Meanings -- a malignant phenomenon

Dormant meanings are sometimes difficult to recognize. Yet in their dormant, unrecognized state they may continue to thrive. At some future moment they may become active in quite surprising, and sometimes lethal ways.

The careers of Primo Levi and Jerzy Kosinski,[37] two well-known Holocaust survivors, again come to mind. After surviving the Holocaust each became a distinguished writer. Each seemed to have found a way to live an effective and productive life after surviving their ordeal at the hands of the Nazis. Rather than wallowing in impotent depression they found ways to be creative. Instead of continually harping on the horrors they had known, they wrote insightfully and rewardingly about life's promises and joys (while also writing insightfully about the horrors). Yet each of them eventually committed suicide. Despite their apparent success at surmounting survivor guilt, they ended their lives with their own hands. It seems that their present life was beyond meaning or, its meaning was so clouded with torment that it could no longer be embraced.

Did they, and several other survivors who became successful writers who eventually committed suicide believe that they did not deserve to live because of their success? How might this have operated? A plausible sequence follows: As their writing found a wide audience they received wide acclaim. They received awards. They attained a measure of financial security. They gained fame. All this came at a price which, in the case of Primo Levi, has been documented. Roughly stated, the response amounted to the haunting question: Do my successes mean that I am dancing on the grave of those who did not survive? Am I enjoying success because they did not survive? In this way of thinking each new success – each new award, each new acclaim for one's work – is regarded as more guilt-provoking failure. In this process the largely dormant survivor guilt actually continues to grow. It is fed by one's current, everyday experiences. Finally, it explodes into the open with the demand to put an end to this miserable life.

Stated differently, in their productive lives these highly successful writers seemed to have overcome what we generally call survivor guilt. Yet this might only have been a surface phenomenon – their "First Path." The reality may have been that their survivor guilt remained. It was largely hidden, even from these writers' own awareness. It was dormant – in a "Second Path." And more importantly, in that dormant state it could continue to grow – fed, perversely, by their current "successes" – culminating in a malignant explosion of these unmentionables that gave life untenable meaning.

I first became aware of the dormant growth of potentially poisonous culture components while reviewing historic episodes of anti-Semitism. In the early twentieth century it was believed that anti-Semitism was a rather primitive practice that had disappeared from Europe long ago. It had culminated in the Crusades and the Inquisition and had surely been laid to rest by the rise of Modernism, where life's meaning is defined by rationality, which is the antithesis of religious or ethnic zealotry. Nations such as Germany, the very embodiment of Modernism, had surely surpassed primitive anti-Semitism. Surely a truly modern country such as Germany would not abide crude anti-Semitism.

In reality, it now seems anti-Semitism had not been eliminated from the culture repertoire of Germany. The explosion of the most extreme form of anti-Semitism in Germany suggests something quite different from what Modernism had led us to expect. Namely, that during the period before the Nazi era in Germany, anti-Semitism may merely have been dormant, not eradicated. In that dormant state – no longer visible and subject to public scrutiny and regulation – anti-Semitism could grow into extreme configurations, and these were available for activation by Hitler and his retinue of Nazis.

Another case of malignant dormant meaning:

The issue of malignant dormancies interfering with the life of individuals is not confined to Jews and the Holocaust. Clarence Page, an African-American journalist, wrote about his first wife, Lea, also an African-American journalist.[38] She was born in appalling urban ghetto circumstances. Through sheer determination, discipline, and effort she succeeded in leaving the ghetto and becoming a distinguished journalist, with many awards and much pubic acclaim coming her way. Yet she continued to feel torn by conflict – toward the white world and also toward the world of African-Americans where, she felt, a "successful" person simply did not fit. She committed suicide.

It seems that the dormant sense of guilt became increasingly potent even as its bearer became more "successful" at overcoming cultural obstacles to living an effective and rewarding life. It culminated, finally, in the activation of this dormant cancer in a virulent, life-denying form. It seems that while this woman grew to become more and more successful, the guilt about succeeding also grew, albeit in dormant form, until it finally erupted with lethal force, just as it may have done for Primo Levi and

Jerzy Kosinsky. (I have picked just three cases, although more cases exist. Marilyn Monroe comes to mind: her public adoration did not keep her from eventually taking an overdose of sleeping pills.)

Is there a process by which an occasional monster within us is being fed even while its obverse twin – the successful, life-affirming individual – appears to win? Was Lea Page under greater pressure than the pre-civil rights movement Uncle Tom who smilingly accepted racial humiliation? She surely operated under a different set of meanings than Uncle Tom did, one that stated that, for African-Americans, second-class citizenship is not acceptable. Did she assiduously, by the minute, recognize, respond to, and place in storage every single racial humiliation that persisted and came her way? She presumably kept account in a very different way from any Uncle Tom. In her life a different process was at work, one that included a multiplier effect to each humiliation, whereas within Uncle Tom there operated a dissipating effect that enabled him to accept humiliation without loss of dignity. The Uncle Tom type of adaptation to humiliation was often made possible by immersion in a strong religious community, where one's dignity did not depend on one's standing in the white community.

In the cases I have mentioned a sense of guilt is shorthand for a sense of dissonance in the individual's ongoing life, creating an unlivable world for that individual. In psychology there is an entire body of research on cognitive dissonance that bears on this situation. In the cases I mentioned, all options for living seem untenable, once they come out into the open.

By contrast, in seems that when one element of the individual's psychological life is dormant – silent, but continuing to exist – the degree of dissonance can grow to unmanageable and unlivable levels. The dormant element is rarely subject to reality testing and control, even while it continues to silently grow and grow. It can become an obverse twin lodged within the outwardly successful individual. When it finally erupts into the open, it can have life-destroying consequences.

Exuberant Meaning: Visit to an Opera

While listening to the tragic ending of Giacomo Puccini's La Bohème, who would not be prepared to give one's life if only Mimi could live? Exists there a person so cold who would not gladly make this sacrifice, or at least fantasize doing so? Who, on witnessing an outstanding performance of this opera, does not feel connected to that world of poor artists? Not only connected, but embraced by something exuberantly meaningful, all triggered by experiencing this artistic masterpiece.

"Exuberantly meaningful" – just what does that mean? What meaning is being brought to life? The answer will differ for each of us. To one person, it is the sweetness of love; to another, life's vulnerability; to yet another, selflessness, fate, nirvana, and unblemished bliss. Many more vital reference points could be listed. Each of us discovers a personal version of exuberant embrace, depending on what meaning we individually hold most dear and vulnerable.

The actual plot of this opera could scarcely be less earthshaking. It gives a snapshot of the struggling lives of young artists – their poverty, petty quarrels, and efforts to do creative work amid a world of hardship and annoyances, such as landlords who insist on being paid the rent. What transforms this potentially dreary scene into a shatteringly powerful experience is the artistry being brought to bear – how the story is told and, most of all, by the music and its performance.

This combination of a story combined with unexcelled artistry creates a connection for us while we sit in the theater. It unites us with some of the most profoundly personal yearnings we envision for our own lives. How does this work? The performance – taking place in a particular configuration of social space – creates a heightened vision of our purest yearnings and aspirations. We sense that we are in touch with something profoundly meaningful. We feel we have gained access to it, here and now, at least for this moment. Of course what is meaningful may differ for each one of us.

However, an artistic performance gives us access to something profoundly important to ourselves *in a very privileged way.* We "experience" the sense of access to this meaningful message without having to do anything about it. After we leave the theater we are under no obligation to live up to the awakened sensibility of what is most important to us. We can leave it all behind after we have applauded the opera's performance. On the other hand, the awakening may indeed have a lasting impact on how we henceforth lead our lives. But the performance itself cannot ensure that we will do so.

What applies to this opera – and to any opera, and to any artistic experience – is that its message is undefined in this particular configuration of social space. It is up to the individual recipient to clarify the meaningful message. The great advantage is that we can, and must, tailor the meaningful message to our own needs, concerns, and capabilities. There is virtually no limit to the variety of meanings we can derive. Puccini has no control whatsoever over the meaning you derive from his masterpiece. This goes for all artists, once their work is handed over to the public domain.

The negative side of this that any implementation of a message, even a clarification of what the message means, is left up to the vagaries of personal whim. There are no directives as to what to do after receiving an artistic message. There is no obligation to transform one's life on the basis of the message. How many people have purified their lives after hearing this opera? We have no way of knowing. Even those who were deeply moved by it, only the smallest number of persons are likely to change their lives.

Stated differently, this (and any) opera offers a very short-lived transformation to the listener. It usually leaves very little, if any, residue. There is no imperative to incorporate the new access to one's profoundest yearnings and convictions into action – not now, tomorrow or thereafter.

By contrast, when you receive a "scientific" message from your doctor – that you had better make certain changes in your eating habits because of a connection to your current health – you are under obligation to accept the message and to implement it. It comes from a very different social space. It impinges on your life in a far more direct and decisive way. It produces something far more focused and authoritative than the artistic message. It gives fewer choices than the artistic message. It mandates that the correlation to your health requires specific action. The impact on your life is direct and explicit.

The opera's impact, so powerful and transcendent in its vision, contains no imperatives. Its profound vision is a brief mirage that you have admired because it has shaken you beautifully and profoundly. You will surely see this opera again. It will again move you. But you will again consider yourself entertained rather than instructed. You will again do nothing to implement its message.

Meanings: Lost, Dissipated and Retained

Who remembers the deliberate starvation deaths of about thirteen million Kulaks in Stalin's Soviet Union? Who thought we would ever forget Pearl Harbor after hearing, for so many years, *Remember Pearl Harbor*! Can American Southerners forget the legacy of the Confederacy?

I am about to raise more questions than give good answers. Still, it is important to consider the questions.

One singular historical event – real or imagined – can produce meanings that will permeate a social space. These meanings may, on occasion, pervade most of a community's culture and ongoing life – then seemingly be eradicated and forgotten, only to periodically resurface, sometimes with awesome fury. (As you may have guessed, as a Jew, I am referring to anti-Semitism's history over centuries. But I could equally have referred to other recurrent inter-religious and inter-ethnic horrors.)

Another event, perhaps equally singular, leaves only the vaguest residue in subsequent life. As far as we know, there is little congruence between the profundity of an event and its afterlife residue of meanings. A fairly trivial event may enjoy a rich afterlife, whereas a powerful event may fade utterly, leaving no trace.

What is more, emanating meanings from singular events can produce highly unpredictable results. I am reminded of the antagonisms between Croats and Serbs in the former Yugoslavia. There, the mass atrocities by Croats against Serbs during the Nazi era did not produce revulsion against mass atrocities. Instead, there followed mass atrocities by Serbs against Croats as soon as the opportunity arose some decades later.

Emanations from a singular even can produce impact that is real and profound. An eminent philosopher, the late Robert Nozick of Harvard University, said this about the emanating meaning from the Holocaust: "Humanity has lost its claim to continue…we are all stained [by it]."[39] To Christians he says, "The Holocaust has shut the door that Christ opened… nullifying the redemption out of humanity's fallen state [given through Christ]"; "The Christian era has closed…The human species is now de-sanctified; if it were ended or obliterated now, its end would no longer constitute a special tragedy… The Holocaust is a massive cataclysm that distorts everything around it."

Robert Nozick reminds us that in the Holocaust humans enacted a level of evil – of cruelty, murder, and assault on human dignity – that surpassed all others in known human experience. This event, the philosopher tells us, has stained all of us. It made and still has singular impact on all human endeavors.

In terms of the orientation I am developing here, one can rephrase the philosopher's statement. Namely, that the Holocaust has fundamentally transformed our social space. That space now contains a pervasive, unmatched denigration of the meaning of human life. According to Nozick, nothing whatsoever in the life of our species can escape that impact.

I am here reporting this philosopher's view. I am not sure that, in the long run, it will prove to be true. Nonetheless, it is an important insight.

Its pessimism is reflective of other times and places. For example, after World War I it was thought that its horrors left such ghastly memories, such revulsion against warfare, that there surely would be consensus to make every effort to create a more peaceful world. Wars should be, and would be outlawed. To implement this message there was the creation of The League of Nations, an international effort to do just that. It failed. After the Second World there was, similarly, revulsion against warfare, now taking place in its more modern format. In order to implement an anti-war message, there followed the creation of the United Nations. It, too, failed to prevent further carnage.

What is the real "meaning" in all of this? Perhaps Nozick's view – of the permanently denigrated meaning of human life – is even more pervasive than mere post-Holocaust revulsion. Does it say something about the very meaning of human life imbedded in the DNA of our human species? If the denigration of human life is so fundamental, then it seems only reasonable that our species has merely been granted temporary reprieve – until we perfect even more efficient ways of killing one another?

I cannot bear to end this discussion on such a pessimistic note. A recent book by the columnist Thomas Friedman (titled, "Thanks for being late: An optimistic guide to Thriving in an age of Acceleration") suggests that at least one influential, sensitive person believes in a different meaning prevailing in our social space. His theme is that we need not succumb to a Nozickian pessimism (he does not use this particular term) but, instead, subscribe to pervasive and powerful *human adaptability*. This has resulted in many instances of flexibility and benign growth in the face of adversity. Its modern version, surely, is the emergence of highly productive science.

In this book I, also, hope to bring an optimistic vision. Namely that viable social behavior sciences are achievable, and may yet avert our species' lurch toward extinction. Yes, we humans killed over 100 million of our fellow-humans during this past century. And since then we have developed even more efficient ways of killing one another. And if we continue on our present course, we may indeed succeed in extinguishing our species.

All this ignores that we live in a golden age of successful science, especially the physical and genetic sciences. This demonstrates optimism about our capacity to cope with the conditions under which we humans live. Perhaps even more importantly, it says much about the human capacity to create viable science. Can we create a viable science about social space before it is too late to save our species? It took four centuries – since Newton – to develop the level of sophistication of modern physics. Yet the DNA-based genetic sciences are fairly new, and developing very rapidly. We don't necessarily have to wait four centuries to create viable science about human life in social space.

Yes, the human social behavior sciences are not nearly as sophisticated as the other sciences. Compared to physics and its science about physical space, our science about social space is at a pre-Newton level. Nor have we reached the refinement of DNA-based genetic biology. But the posture to create viable science is the same. The theoretical physicist Henry Margenau suggested that the most basic tools of science are constructs. It consists of combining observation of what exists in nature together with deliberate mental leaps – in the form of invented constructs that make sense of what exists in nature. Gravitation and Relativity in physics, the Periodic Table and Valence in chemistry, DNA and Chromosomes in biology and genetics are such constructs. And so, in a preliminary way, are my suggested Four Aspects of Social Space. We may yet find a faster way to achieve viability than even DNA-based genetic biology. We have nothing to lose but our shackles. And everything to gain, perhaps even preventing our species' lurch to extinction.

CONCLUSION

This book is the fourth one of a quartet of books in my Holocaust survivor's Odyssey. All address both my own survival of the Holocaust, where my parents, my brother and many other relatives were murdered, and the realization, as a sociologist, that viable science of human social behavior is desperately needed. And is feasible. Given sufficient use of our imagination, we can create it. Alfred North Whitehead taught us that science is adventure of the mind. I have tried to be guided by that perspective. Yes, there is the very real danger that our human species may be lurching toward self-destruction. And as I mentioned previously, during the past century we humans killed over 100 million of our fellow human beings. And that since then we have developed every-more efficient ways of killing one another. Yes, the challenge is real. But so can be our response.

The first two books in the quartet – "Ordinary People and Extraordinary Evil," and "Confronting Evil" – address the Holocaust in ways that most historians and writers of personal memoirs do not address it. Explicitly or implicitly, these writers focus on its uniqueness. From the point of view of its victims and their relatives the Holocaust is, of course, terribly unique. But we cannot afford to regard it as unique if we are going to learn from it, and derive prophylactic information from it. To do so we need to adopt a generalizing, science perspective to it. This I attempt to do in these two books.

The next two books come from my conviction that, for me, writing about – and wrestling with – the Holocaust is not enough. Call it survivor guilt, I believe I must address wider issues about human social co-existence. The two resulting books use virtually the same data and examples from day-to-day living. But their focus is entirely different. The first book, "Immediacy: Our ways of Coping in Everyday Life" tries to foster a science of social psychology based on human coping behavior. The present book is focused on creating science about Social Space, the "post-partum womb" I mentioned at the beginning of this book. It is where we live and how we live. In it – this "Living in Social Space" – is an amalgam of our own making and our social context. It is here, inviting to be explored.

What have we learned about the "post-partum womb" we inhabit? For response, I'll resort to the perspective of physicists. If you ask a physicist, What is the nature of physical space? He /or she is apt to answer by mentioning some *constructs* – such as Gravitation and Relativity – that are critical aspects of what is known about the nature of physical space. They are building blocks which over centuries (in the case of Newton's Law of Universal Gravitation) produced the rich science we know as modern physics. In that spirit I suggested four constructs about aspects of human social space. These might eventually be building blocks for more sophisticated science about Social Space. The constructs I have presented are: *Hidden Space* – and the resultant Second Path phenomenon // *Closed Space* – and the resultant Moral World phenomenon // *Transcendent Space* – and the resultant access-to-the-Ultimate phenomenon // *Meaningful Space* – and the resultant creation of meaning phenomenon. The text you have read provides some illustrative material of how these actually manifest themselves.

My use of these constructs is not nearly as quantitatively sophisticated as those created by physicists about physical space. But I am convinced that they stand in the same tradition of creating serious science by proposing viable constructs. My hope is that the constructs I proposed might be building blocks for such science or, at least, be precursors of such science.

NOTES

1   Myriam Anissimor, *Primo Levi: Tragedy of an Optimist*. New York: The Overlook Press, 1999. P. 383.

2   Ibid., p. 405.

3   Ibid.

4   Aired on December 3, 1996.

5   Walter Bruegemann, "The Struggle Toward Reconciliation," in Bill Moyers, editor, *Talking about Genesis: A Resource Guide* (New York: Doubleday, 1996). Copyright Public Affairs Television.

6   Ibid., p. 133.

7   Glenn Loury, "The Crisis of Color Consciousness," *The Washington Post*, July 21, 1996.

8   Paul M. Barrett, *The Good Black: A True Story of Race in America*. (New York: Dutton, 1998). See also Ellis Cose, *The Rage of a Privileged Class: Why are middle-class blacks angry? Why should America care?* (New York: Harper Collins, 1993).

    Here is a wider perspective: On August 30, 2008, Will Herbert, a New York Times columnist, wrote, "…with Barack Obama formally accepting the Democratic presidential nomination…I talked to black residents in and around Detroit…The message I heard again and again was that the triumph of Senator Obama in securing the nomination helped to redeem some of the disappointment and grief of many years of racial humiliation and oppression."

9   Ibid., p. 162.

10 Ibid., p. 117.

11 Ibid., p. 5.

12 Cited from *Time* magazine, February 24, 1997, p. 27.

13 George Lee Butler, "Scrap nuclear weapons – all of them," *The Baltimore Sun*, February 4, 1997. This article is adapted from a speech given on January 8, 1997, at the Henry L. Stimson Center in Washington.

[14] Ibid.

[15] "Tapes that show LBJ tormented by escalation of war," *The Baltimore Sun*, February 15, 1997.

[16] Ibid.

[17] Ibid.

[18] For an intriguing look at "time," see Alan Lightman, *Einstein's Dreams* (New York: Warner Books, 1993).

[19] Magoroh Maruyama, "The Second Cybernetics: Deviation-Amplifying Mutual Causal Processes," in Fred Emil Katz, editor, *Contemporary Sociological Theory* (New York: Random House, 1971). In the editorial section I propose a Third and a Fourth Cybernetics. (FEK)

[20] Stanley Milgram, *Obedience to Authority: An Experimental View* (New York: Harper and Row, 1974).

[21] Christopher Browning, *Ordinary Men: Reserve Battalion 101 and the Final Solution in Poland* (New York: Harper Perennial, 1993).

[22] Milgram, *Obedience to Authority*, pp. 20-21.

[23] "Epilogue," Milgram, *Obedience to Authority*.

[24] Ibid., p. 148.

[25] Milgram himself uses this term. He follows the formulation of Erving Goffman in his book, *The Presentation of Self in Everyday Life* (New York: Doubleday Anchor Books, 1959). My use of the term differs somewhat from theirs. They focus on how the individual feels the moral constraint of one's sense of self.

[26] Milgram, *Obedience to Authority*, p. 10.

[27] Ibid.

[28] Fred Emil Katz, *Ordinary People and Extraordinary Evil: A Report on the Beguilings of Evil* (Albany, NY: State Univesity of New York Press, 1993).

[29] I am indebted to an article on this issue by Susan B. Glasser and Steve Coll, "The Web as Weapon," that appeared in *The Washington Post*, August 9, 2005.

[30] Viktor E. Frankl, *Man's Search for Meaning: An Introduction to Logotherapy*, 3rd ed. (New York: Simon and Schuster, Touchstone Books, 1984).

[31] Ibid., p. 78

32 Fred Emil Katz, *Autonomy and Organization: The Limits of Social Control* (New York: Random House, 1968); Fred Emil Katz, *Structuralism in Sociology* (Albany, NY State Univesity of New York Press, 19760, ch. 3.

33 Freud cites his friend Roman Rolain as saying that the core or religiosity is "a feeling which he would like to call a sensation of 'eternity' – a feeling of something limitless, unbounded…it is a source of religious energy." (Sigmund Freud, *Civilization and its Discontents* [New York: W. W. Norton, 1961], p. 11.) This "feeling" comes very close to what I am calling the sense of transcendence. However, I must add that Freud immediately attacked his friend's idea.

34 Robert Burrus, "The divine irony of the last laugh," *The Sun* (Baltimore), May 14, 1997, p. 11A.

35 See Fred Emil Katz, *Autonomy and Organization: The Limits of Social Control* (New York: Random House, 1968); Fred Emil Katz, *Structuralism in Sociology: An Approach to Knowledge* (Albany, NY: SUNY Press, 1976).

36 This is based on the study by Robert J. Lifton, *The Nazi Doctors: Medical Killing and the Psychology of Genocide* (New York: Basic Books, 1986).

37 I discussed these writers in the chapter "We divide ourselves."

38 Clarence Page, "Survivor guilt: the angst of the black bourgeoisie, The Sun (Baltimore), March 11, 1996.

39 Robert Nozick, *The Examined Life* (New York: Simon and Schuster, 1988), pp. 238-141.
    This essay is an adaptation of a chapter titled "The World of Links – And the Dynamics of Immediacy," in Fred Emil Katz, Immediacy: *How our world confronts us & How we confront our world* (Baltimore: Discern Books, 2003). Copyright Fred Emil Katz. It is used here by permission.

INDEX

Puccini, Giacomo 94

R

Racism 11, 28, 76
Reserve Battalion 42, 43, 104
Roosevelt, Franklin vii

S

Second Path xii, xiii, 1, 2, 3, 4, 5, 6,
    7, 8, 10, 11, 13, 14, 15, 16, 17,
    18, 19, 20, 21, 23, 24, 25, 26,
    91, 102
Sexuality 2, 12, 13, 14, 67, 83, 85
Soviet Union 48, 74, 89, 96
Suicide 2, 3, 4, 17, 24, 30, 44, 45, 54,
    63, 64, 66, 91, 92
Survivor guilt 3, 4, 91, 101, 105, 112

T

Terrorism 30
Transcendence 54, 56, 57, 58, 61, 62,
    63, 66, 67, 68, 78, 79, 80, 105
Transcendent Space 63, 68, 102

U

Ultimates 45, 68, 80, 81
Unmentionables xiii, 1, 2, 6, 7, 11, 12,
    13, 14, 15, 17, 18, 19, 20, 21, 23,
    24, 25, 26, 91
U. S. Army 15

V

Vietnam 19, 20, 34, 35
Vietnam war 19, 20, 34

W

Whitehead, A. vii, 82, 101, 111
Wirths, Eduard 76
World War I 71, 88, 98

Z

Zarqawi, Abu Musab 44

Acknowledgement

This book bears the imprint of my teachers. At the University of North Carolina at Chapel Hill the ebullient Harvey Smith taught a generation of students a love for "doing" sociology. Sociology was a calling, a religion, a unique perspective on this world of ours. Also at Chapel Hill was Rupert Vance, a man crippled by polio who, although unable to walk, was able to soar. He helped his students to also soar. At Guilford College, my undergraduate alma mater, Edna Weiss attempted to teach me English grammar. And she encouraged me to write. Robert Dinkel and David Stafford introduced me to sociology – its humane concerns and its glimmer of science. And Frederick Crownfield. He introduced me to the work of Alfred North Whitehead, his teacher at Harvard. Crownfield's wayward thinking contributed to whatever creativity you may find in this book.

I am grateful to my father. He showed me that dreams can be a lifeline, a sustaining haven amid turbulence. Dreams did so for him while the Nazi persecution first destroyed his livelihood and eventually his life, giving him some serenity amid that engulfing journey.

I am grateful to my mother. She gave me life twice. First in 1927, in the traditional way. Then in 1939, arranging my escape to England, away from the Holocaust horrors in Germany. Between these years she contributed boundless love to my life. It has helped to sustain me to this day.

In England, I was found by Hertha Karger. Her London home became a launching pad toward finding new life for a number of Jewish refugees from Nazi Germany, adults as well as orphaned children, as I was, who needed an adult's kindly touch and guidance. Speaking of guidance, in the Karger home I met the widow of Paul Ehrlich, who won the Nobel Prize for the medical discovery he called "606," which followed 605 failures. His stubborn faith in science and intuition stayed with me and kept me going past many rejections of my earlier work. Above my desk I keep this sign: "606."

In America, there was Ada Field, my feisty landlady at Guilford College. She made it possible for me to attend graduate school in Chapel Hill, when I had absolutely no money. In her personal life she demonstrated that one person can make a difference in how countries conduct their affairs. She, a tiny woman in her seventies, actively promoted better government. (Senator Sam Ervin, of Watergate fame, was one of her "boys" she instructed on how they should be conducting their political lives. He visited her. And listened.) My book is not as practical as Ada Field's work. But it surely benefited from her sense of the need to get a better grip on how we humans conduct ourselves.

Finally, I acknowledge that for me, clarifying the nature of Social Space is personal and urgent. It is my effort to both continue my response to genocides – that claimed the life of my parents and my brother – and our living in a whirlwind of connectivity, where our lack of grounding can be disconcerting and dangerous. I bring to it the dubious gift of survivor guilt, which drives my need to address genocides in new ways – I tried to do so in two books, *Ordinary People and Extraordinary Evil,* and *Confronting Evil* – and address the very real possibility that our species is lurching toward extinction if we don't achieve a far more viable science about Social Space, in and through which we live.

Sophisticated science cannot be achieved overnight. It took physicists centuries – since Newton, to be exact – to develop physics as sophisticated as it is today. Underlying that success is the realization that science is more than observation of what exists in nature. Science is adventure of the mind. It took many creative leaps of the mind to produce science as advanced as modern physics, chemistry, and genetic biology. This book suggests some creative leaps – in the form of four constructs – to help us understand the Social Space in which we live our lives. They are surely not the last word of a viable science about Social Space. But they may just be the tantalizing groping that illuminates, and encourages others to go further. Read, and enjoy the adventure.

And also, a hearty thank you to Jean Lillquist for her patient and powerful help in editing this book.

****

This book is a revised version of a previous book, "Our quest for effective living," also published by AuthorHouse.

www.ingramcontent.com/pod-product-compliance
Lightning Source LLC
Chambersburg PA
CBHW020537290526
45786CB00002B/917